GALILEO COPERNICUS FARADAY WREN HELMHOLTZ MENDELEYEV FRANKLIN

MUSEUM OF SCIENCE AND INDUSTRY

CHICAGO

DESCARTES HALE NEWTON GIBBS EUCLID ARCHIMEDES KELVIN ARISTOTLE

TER GUTENBERG DARWIN HENRY DALTON PASTEUR BERNARD HARVEY HILL

DA VINCI   CLAUSIUS   PERRONET   SUESS   HIPPOCRATES   BUCH   ICTINUS   MARC

SOLVAY HAMILTON PERKIN AGASSIZ NASMYTH BUNSEN AGRICOLA JOULE

LAMARCK DESMAREST HAÜY ARRHENIUS CHAMBERLIN HUTTON EDISON BES

MER CURIE LEEUWENHOEK DAVY WHITNEY LEGENDRE AVOGADRO SMEATON

Jay Pridmore

Museum of Science and Industry, Chicago

HARRY N. ABRAMS, INC., PUBLISHERS

IN ASSOCIATION WITH THE

MUSEUM OF SCIENCE AND INDUSTRY,

CHICAGO

Contents

FOR THE MUSEUM OF SCIENCE AND INDUSTRY
President and CEO: Dr. James S. Kahn
Director of New Ventures: Christy Overgard
Associate of New Ventures: Alycia Wright

FOR HARRY N. ABRAMS, INC.
Project Manager: James Leggio
Associate Editor: Margaret Donovan
Designer: Judith Hudson

LIBRARY OF CONGRESS
CATALOGING-IN-PUBLICATION DATA
Pridmore, Jay.
Museum of Science and Industry, Chicago /
Jay Pridmore.
     p.   cm.
Includes bibliographical references and index.
ISBN 0-8109-4289-5 (cloth)
ISBN 0-8109-2672-5 (mus. pbk.)
1. Museum of Science and Industry
(Chicago, Ill.) 2. Museum of Science and
Industry (Chicago, Ill.)—Pictorial works.
I. Museum of Science and Industry
(Chicago, Ill.) II. Title.
T180.C45M873 1996
607.4'773'11—dc20   96-2829

The Museum of Science and Industry has enchanted, educated, and endeared itself to well over 150 million guests since its opening in 1933. Founded by the generosity, vision, and wisdom of Julius Rosenwald and fashioned after the Deutsches Museum in Munich, the Museum is situated in beautiful Jackson Park, steps away from Lake Michigan in the Hyde Park section of Chicago. From its inception, the Museum has been dedicated to the advancement of scientific literacy. Housed in a historic Beaux-Arts building with an Art Deco interior, its hundreds of exhibits are displayed throughout 750,000 square feet of space.

Since 1987 the staff of the Museum has been engaged in the monumental task of implementing a strategic plan named MSI 2000, dedicated to defining the Museum's educational philosophy, refurbishing its halls with new exhibits, and restoring its physical plant. With the successful completion of the MSI 2000 campaign, this book has been developed to capture, communicate, and celebrate the new energy within the Museum. Its photographs record our landmark facade and the great "icons" within our vast halls, as well as the details that often escape notice in a museum of this size. The book takes you behind the scenes so that we can reveal to you the creative inner workings of exhibits under development; simultaneously, we have captured you, the visitor, your expressions and impressions, which continue to inspire us: your curiosity, absorption, excitement, and joy of discovery. The text provides a historical chronicle that traces the development of each Museum Zone through a series of vignettes. In this way, we have tried to underscore the special challenge an institution based on science, industry, and technology faces – to maintain timely, topical exhibits for visitors of all ages.

We hope that you enjoy this fresh look at our Museum and that your return visits will permit you to share our continuing evolution through the coming years!

Dr. James S. Kahn
President and CEO
Museum of Science and Industry

Foreword

When the Museum of Science and Industry opened its doors in 1933, it had been seven years in the planning. Its founders could have used more time – only a small portion of the interior was complete even then – but the city, like the nation, was impatient to see what they had wrought. The Museum was to fill a huge and magnificent building, and its mission was grander still: to explore the unfolding destiny of the modern industrial world.

That destiny lay in technology, in the scientific and mechanical advances that were altering society in previously inconceivable ways. Inventions such as the airplane and the radio were only just then becoming familiar parts of modern life. Nuclear energy was already on the horizon. Calculating machines were evolving and giving the first sense that eventually they might come to resemble the human brain. In these and in many other areas, technological change was rushing forward with the growing momentum of a revolution.

Industrialization was a global phenomenon, of course, but it came with particular force to Chicago. By then America's second-largest city, Chicago was still growing at an astonishing rate, its progress driven especially by inventors and engineers. In the previous century, the railroads had made Chicago a great industrial hub. Later, its innovative architecture and its modern power plants transformed it into what contemporary historians called the first great city of the modern age. Circumstances had conspired to create an urban center of great size and rare power.

Introduction

Chicagoans themselves were well aware of the magnitude of the changes that were emerging, and many understood they were seeing history take place before their eyes. It was natural, therefore, for many residents to imagine a monument to the driving force behind such burgeoning growth. A museum, some thought, could elucidate the modern world, and even point to changes that the future certainly had in store.

This was the dynamic spark for the Museum of Science and Industry. While museums of all kinds were noble institutions, most were dedicated to quiet contemplation of people and things past. This one, the founders believed, would be different. Their museum would be no series of dusty spaces, glass cases, and exhibitions frozen in time. Technology was something in motion; in this museum, locomotives might whistle, printing presses clatter, dynamos whirl. As other great museums enshrined icons of ancient Egypt or masterpieces of the Renaissance, this one would celebrate the wonders of internal combustion and electromagnetism.

Most of all, this one would be a museum of progress. History would play its role here with exhibits devoted to the landmark inventions of James Watt and Thomas Edison. But the world's greatest wonders, the founders agreed, rose from newer developments – in energy, transportation, medicine, and many other fields. Thus, the Museum of Science and Industry would address above all the future. To crystallize the discoveries of science, to explain the implications of new technology – this became its mission. It would demonstrate the workings of modern mechanics and explicate the laws of physics. Most intriguing of all was the possibility that the Museum might go further still and touch a future that was unrealized but inevitable.

This challenge – for a museum to comprehend technology and keep pace with progress – quickly captured the imagination of the public, and the Museum of Science and Industry became one of the most talked-about institutions of its era. It generated not only excitement and curiosity but also impatience. "When will it be finished?" asked the reporters who covered the story.

The founders' answer was "Never!" and it was a perfectly reasonable response. Elaborate exhibitions could show how airplanes flew and industrial processes worked, but behind the hard technologies on display was a deeper theme that underlay everything else. The Museum of Science and Industry was to be about the nature of human ingenuity, constantly taking new forms. It was a place to come and see technological creativity revealing itself in new advances of industrial progress.

This human dimension, the delicate relationship between people and machines, became the true and enduring theme of the Museum. By understanding that relationship, its founders believed, the Museum could go beyond being a repository of past history and assume a role that most museums never dared. The founders hoped that by looking into the inventive potential of the present, the institution might influence the direction of the future. It was not a modest ambition.

THE FOUNDING OF THE MUSEUM

The idea for a museum devoted to science and industry came from a Chicagoan who was one of the era's great philanthropists. Julius Rosenwald, president of Sears, Roebuck & Company, discerned that modern society was very much under the influence of rising technologies. A man of enormous wealth and uncommon vision, Rosenwald observed that the nation's continued welfare depended upon greater understanding of those potent forces.

For several years, Rosenwald had imagined a museum to promote such understanding. As he later recounted, the idea went back to a vacation trip that he had taken with his family to Munich in 1916. There he visited relatives and made the rounds of that city's rich cultural institutions. Munich's museums of art and natural history were magnificent, Rosenwald remembered, but the deepest impression on him was made by a relatively new institution, the Deutsches Museum, which chronicled Europe's industrial progress.

Rosenwald recalled most of all the enthusiasm of his youngest son, William, who was 14 at the time and understandably fatigued by the days of sightseeing – until they reached the Deutsches Museum. There, William was enthralled by many fascinating exhibits, with moving parts and stimulating sounds, such as models of steam engines and a miniature blast furnace, activated by cranks and push buttons. The Deutsches Museum energized William's eager young mind as the others had not, and this lesson was not lost on his father.

A few years later, Rosenwald learned that the idea for a new industrial museum was not his alone. In 1924, serious plans were being laid to create a National Museum of Engineering and Industry in Washington, D.C. This new museum would illustrate and explain, according to its organizational literature, the "phenomenal acceleration of industrial progress that commenced with the opening of the present century." Moreover, it would expand beyond its parent organization, the Smithsonian Institution in Washington, with branch museums planned for New York, focused on electrical progress; for Pittsburgh, on the steel industry; and for Chicago, with the "world's greatest assemblage of agricultural implements."

17

Rosenwald quickly pledged a $1-million donation for this museum. The project was soon slowed by a tangle of competing interests, but the Sears, Roebuck magnate maintained a strong interest in the idea for such an institution. Then in 1926, Rosenwald received national press attention with the announcement that he was prepared to donate $3 million toward the creation of an industrial museum in Chicago. Other cities had shown interest in establishing their own museums as well, also independent of the Smithsonian, but only Chicago could point to a commitment of cold cash sufficient to make its dream a reality.

As savvy as he was wealthy, Rosenwald quickly enlisted the support of the Commercial Club of Chicago, which included the city's industrial and business elite. A number of members – including the presidents of Illinois Bell, the Pullman Company, and the First National Bank of Chicago – agreed to sit on an organizing committee for the museum. This provided the project with the broad base of support that was needed. The newspapers fostered enthusiasm for the project with favorable articles and editorials, and politicians predictably jumped on the bandwagon as well. Indeed, Rosenwald's proposal seemed very much in tune with the city's sense of itself – Chicago's very name seemed synonymous with industrial progress. And nearly as important to this groundswell of interest was a palpable sense of civic pride that this city could succeed in museum building where all other American cities had failed.

The World's Columbian Exposition of 1893 was essentially a city of temporary structures built to be dismantled after the fair ended. Among its great plaster pavilions, only the Palace of Fine Arts, which had a brick substructure, was not destroyed. It served as the Field Museum from 1893 to 1920, before being renovated for the Museum of Science and Industry.

Inspired by the Deutsches Museum in Munich, Chicago executive and philanthropist Julius Rosenwald founded the Museum of Science and Industry to be America's preeminent leader in informal science education.

The potentially difficult selection of a site for the new museum appeared to be resolved simultaneously with Rosenwald's announcement. It would be the old Palace of Fine Arts, the last remaining major structure from the World's Columbian Exposition of 1893. After the triumphant world's fair, the Field Museum had occupied the building for a while, but the Field had long since left for its new marble home in Grant Park. Never intended to be permanent, the Palace of Fine Arts was now an edifice of crumbling plaster. Despite its magnificent neoclassical architecture, and despite memories of the fair ("Paris on the Prairie," it had been called), there had recently been talk of razing it.

Rosenwald's idea was to restore the Palace of Fine Arts – rebuild it with hard stone, piece by ornamental piece. This reconstruction project, which would require public money as well as Rosenwald's, had enormous appeal to Chicago even beyond the idea of creating a science museum, for it would revive a grand monument of Chicago's past as well as create a major new institution. Among supporters of the concept was Edward Kelly, president of the South Park Commission on whose land the Palace of Fine Arts stood. The backing of Kelly, a future mayor of Chicago, would be essential for the realization of the new museum. Kelly's commission was responsible for a $5-million bond issue that had been approved some years earlier for the purposes of renovating the building.

With politics in mind, Rosenwald sent Kelly and a delegation of other powerful Chicago leaders to Europe to tour the Deutsches Museum in Munich and similar institutions in Vienna and London. When Kelly returned, he was effusive: "The whole German nation is benefited intellectually and Munich is benefited commercially" by the Deutsches Museum. He declared that Chicago should have one too.

19

For the new museum, the plaster
sheathing of the Palace of Fine
Arts was removed, and the exterior
was rebuilt piece by piece with
Bedford limestone, quarried and cut
in Indiana.

20

Despite inspiration from abroad, Chicago's museum would be unique. The European institutions were largely historical, dedicated to a review of past discoveries and inventions. Rosenwald pointed out, in contrast, that contemporary technology should be the focus of this museum. The power of modern science and contemporary industry was of the greatest interest to the people, and could be explained through demonstrations that combined the latest equipment and ideas.

"American inventive genius needs greater stimulation and room for development," Rosenwald told a reporter for the *Chicago Tribune.* "I would like every young growing mind in Chicago to be able to see working models, visualizing developments in machines and processes which have been built by the greatest industrial nation in the world," he said. "In such a museum young Chicago will be able to experience the thrills of going down into the bowels of the earth and see how coal is mined. How many nontechnical people know why their voice carries over the telephone or why the red-hot wires in a glass bottle make electric light?"

As Rosenwald's idea became national news, the continuing flood of publicity was a measure of how deeply the notion of such a museum stirred the public imagination. At the same time, support and advice came from distinguished individuals in many fields, including Max Mason, president of the University of Chicago; George E. Vincent, president of the Rockefeller Foundation; and from a patron saint of American industry, Henry Ford.

The first order of business in staffing the new museum was, quite naturally, to find an executive director. Although the search benefitted from the counsel of many powerful men in this country and around the world, candidates were slow to emerge. C. G. Abbot, secretary of the Smithsonian Institution, answered a friendly inquiry by writing, "As the industrial museum is a comparatively new thing in this country, and is as yet in a stage of development, there are no experienced directors available." Abbot concluded that the Chicago group would have to "develop a man of proper caliber in their own organization."

22 The founders of the Museum of Science and Industry imagined vast interior spaces. "When you come out of that museum," said the first director, Waldemar Kaempffert, "you will have a feeling that you have been part of a vast industrial organism."

LEFT

Limestone figures were created to ornament the frieze above the Museum's main entrance. Each figure, weighing 5 tons and standing 12 feet tall, waited in a storage room as the reconstruction progressed.

BELOW

The figures were lifted and secured into their appropriate spaces during construction. The final effect was meant to recall the architectural grandeur of the Columbian Exposition.

23

It became a gnawing problem: How to find someone capable of translating the visionary goals of the founders into a practical scheme and soon open the doors of a working museum? In the midst of this search, a particularly useful contact was made with Waldemar Kaempffert, science editor of the *New York Times*. Kaempffert was an adept interpreter of technical matters and had recently published a book entitled *A Popular History of American Invention*. Over the course of his career, he witnessed and wrote about advances from hygiene to electric power and even the prospects for space travel.

The trustees on the search committee wrote to Kaempffert, soliciting advice about their problem. Kaempffert replied that the director ought to be someone of "broad cultural outlook and imagination." The ideal person should be something of a humanist as well as a scientist or engineer, with, of course, "organizing ability." It was a tall order, but Kaempffert suggested several candidates, one a professor from the East, another an engineer from the Bureau of Standards in Washington. These and others were considered by the committee in Chicago, but none rose to the top. Only after the trustees began to wonder whether they would ever find someone qualified for the demanding position did they strike upon Kaempffert himself as a candidate. Lucidly communicating the lessons of science was precisely his field; indeed, he had given the search committee a more vivid idea of their own museum simply through his casual correspondence.

Thus did newspaperman Waldemar Kaempffert become the first director of the Museum of Science and Industry. Like Rosenwald, Kaempffert had a deep admiration for the Deutsches Museum and its founding director Dr. Oskar von Miller. "In Munich a student learns more sound engineering in half a day by watching an engine turn a crank shaft than he can in a week by studying the diagrams and descriptions in a textbook," Kaempffert wrote in a *Scientific American* article about the advent of the Chicago museum. Moreover, von Miller, known as the developer of the electrical industry in Germany (that country's "Thomas Edison"), had been greatly successful in coaxing the enthusiastic support of industries throughout Germany for the Deutsches Museum. They contributed real machines to the museum when possible and models when full-size equipment was not. Founded in 1903, the German museum was by this time attracting about a million visitors a year. Kaempffert hoped and expected that American industry, too, would come forward with the machines and money to tell its story, and that the throngs of visitors here would equal those in Munich.

Immediately upon arriving in Chicago in 1928, Kaempffert hired a formidable staff of curators. Scholars and practitioners in chemistry, civil engineering, agriculture, and other fields, they were charged with designing vivid exhibits in a wide range of subjects. Plans began to take shape during a six-month tour by Kaempffert to Munich, Vienna, and other European cities with museums of science and technology. With the lessons of these visits in mind, and after much thought on the subject, Kaempffert and his staff conceived ten "sequences" for the Chicago museum, each filling a large gallery in the spacious building. "The Fundamental Sciences" was planned to be the first among the sequences. It would introduce the principles of physics and chemistry indispensable to understanding subsequent exhibit halls dedicated to geology and mining, power generation, civil engineering, graphic arts, and others.

As curators considered the technical aspects of the sequences, they focused too on a separate question that they regarded as equally important: How could they best dramatize for the public the enormous social implications of technology? The invention of the steam engine, for example, could be viewed as clearly marking the beginning of the Industrial Revolution, the great change that had ushered in the modern age. "James Watt was more than a great inventor," Kaempffert therefore wrote. "He did more to transform the face of the earth and mold social institutions than Alexander the Great, Julius Caesar, and Napoleon Bonaparte." Other early industrial inventions had also had far-reaching consequences. The cotton gin had produced an economy in the American South that contributed to the perpetuation of slavery. And in modern cities, the introduction of elevators led not just to the dramatic architecture of the skyscraper, but also to population densities that many believed unhealthy. Curators thought deeply about how these issues could be presented in engaging and highly visual exhibits.

As its scholarly staff considered these topics from all possible angles, the Museum of Science and Industry was taking on the aura of a university. The curators were publishing articles in journals and corresponding with colleagues around the world. Nevertheless, progress in actually getting the Museum open remained inexplicably slow to the hard-headed businessmen on the board of trustees. This and other problems led to Kaempffert's resignation in 1931. It was a setback which, with the country now deep in the Great Depression, made some people wonder if Chicago's ambitious new museum would ever become a reality. But such fears ultimately proved unwarranted.

26 The Museum's 24 caryatids were
modeled after marble originals from
the porticoes of the Erechtheum on
the Acropolis in Athens.

THE MUSEUM TODAY

The Museum of Science and Industry opened on June 19, 1933. Though it would require a number of years to fill the vast spaces of the splendid building, the essential idea of the Museum, as a place to chronicle and explain technological change, has flourished since then, and it has grown.

At the same time, the founders' early caveat – that such an institution was never truly "finished" – remained true as well. In the early years, it was steam engines and airplanes that told the story of progress, but these were soon overshadowed by newer discoveries and inventions. Television, for example, was sprung on the world in the 1940s and by 1950 became the subject of a memorable exhibit at the Museum in which visitors could watch themselves "live" on screen. More recently, space travel and advanced information-processing systems have taken center stage. And as technology has changed and developed, so has its presentation at the Museum. Today, exhibit halls and programs do not just present the latest technologies, they put them to practical use as well in advanced, often computerized, presentations that help visitors comprehend the vastness of outer space or the complexity of the Information Age.

INTRODUCTION

32

33

INTRODUCTION

The Museum's continuing success in chronicling and explaining scientific development reflects the sustaining vision inherited from its early years. "A real effort must be made to show the people of our country, young and old, the pathway along which we have come to the present stage of our development," said one of the curators in a radio address before the Museum opened. "This is one of the principal functions of the industrial museum: education in social and technical matters, past and present, by the object-lesson method." The imperative, then as today, was to engage the intellectual curiosity of the visitor.

In the early years, curators piqued the interest of youngsters and adults alike with strange and sometimes exotic sights. For example, an opening-day exhibit at the Museum featured a diver in a tank cutting metal with an underwater acetylene torch. Another was an aeronautical training device; visitors could take the controls and guide a model plane through an onrushing current of air. Such demonstrations-in-motion, especially those which invited the visitor's active participation, encouraged people to think about strange and marvelous things, and ask questions of their own.

The continuing importance of this approach is highlighted by the Nobel Prize–winning physicist Dr. Leon Lederman, a trustee of the Museum of Science and Industry. Lederman believes deeply in the power of museums to foster inspired thought. Growing up in New York, he spent much of his own youth visiting the city's museums. Today, as he discusses the problem of education with other eminent scientists, he often asks them about the early influences on their development. Museums are high on almost every list.

35

Bronze relief panels on the Museum's main doors represent the many divisions of science, industry, and technology explored by the Museum.

"A museum is an ideal place to supplement the schools," Lederman says. Museums are needed now more than ever to create an adequate level of "scientific literacy" for everyone, vital in a society increasingly dependent on computers and faced by such real-life threats as AIDS. In this sense, the challenge to the Museum of Science and Industry has grown more difficult, but more important, over time.

To meet these new demands, the Museum's current president, Dr. James S. Kahn, on assuming his post in 1987 began to develop a comprehensive new plan for the institution, one that built on the heritage of the Museum's past, yet reformulated it to meet the future. Among the features of Kahn's plan was the establishment of areas, called "thematic zones," focused on broad subjects such as Energy, Transportation, and Communications. These thematic zones would revitalize Kaempffert's founding idea of "sequences" of exhibit halls and reinforce the Museum's longtime strength as a model for science and technology education. Thematic zones would be designed to attract both schoolchildren and adults to new ideas. Here, cutting-edge scientists and engineers would present the unfolding drama of their work, as each zone would be constantly updated to stay abreast of recent developments.

ABOVE

After its opening in 1933, the Museum was praised for its classical exterior and elaborate Art Deco interior. In the north vestibule, bronze plaques represent Greek gods and goddesses whose realms included science and technology.

RIGHT

Art Deco design elements, like these in a ramp for handicap access, extend into details throughout the Museum.

Also in the new plan, called MSI 2000, was another, more elusive element: the concept of how each thematic zone might fruitfully relate to all the others. As Kahn remarked, "The real challenge is how to connect one exhibit with another. You don't just put up a wall and say, 'You're now going from automobiles to DNA.' You need to ask, 'How do you go from automobiles to the next exhibit hall?'" In other words: How can the Museum build a natural flow through the maze of technology and instill in the visitor a sense of personal discovery? This remains the core of the Museum's purpose. Its initial task may be to convey certain basic information, but its ultimate goal is to encourage visitors to ask questions, combine ideas, and think of new ones. The Museum's galleries are constantly in flux, with new displays and devices, but beyond the hardware and software of the moment lies a continuing commitment to creative thinking itself – to the unrealized possibilities of the scientific imagination.

This museum of the future is a place that fosters new approaches to technological issues – that helps a young visitor to imagine the opportunities of research in space in relation to the needs of human medicine, for example, or the resources of superconductivity applied to the demands of modern transportation. That is the purpose of the Museum of Science and Industry – where groups of wide-eyed children have filled the halls for generations, and where more than a few of them have returned with inventions of their own.

39

I WOULD LIKE EVERY YOUNG GROWING MIND IN CHICAGO TO BE ABLE TO SEE WORKING MODELS, VISUALIZING DEVELOPMENTS

IN MACHINES AND PROCESSES WHICH HAVE BEEN BUILT BY THE GREATEST INDUSTRIAL NATION IN THE WORLD   *Julius Rosenwald*

THROUGH INNOVATIVE AND CREATIVE THINKING, THE MUSEUM STRIVES TO IGNITE VISITORS' CURIOSITY, CHALLENGE

THEIR MINDS, AND ENGAGE THEM IN THE WONDER OF SCIENCE AND TECHNOLOGY   *James S. Kahn*

When asked in 1931 about the nature of his proposed Museum of Science and Industry, founder Julius Rosenwald let his spokesman and attorney, Leo Wormser, give this answer: "The thought is to demonstrate the effect of progress on society. The old idea of a museum as a place of stuffed figures in glass cases is obsolete." Although the Museum was still more than two years away from opening, it was already clear that the physical nature of its exhibits would be highly unorthodox for any museum.

Nowhere was the Rosenwald vision more successfully realized than in an exhibit opened to the public on the Museum's first day: the *Coal Mine,* a dark netherworld with hoist, skip, coal car, and other equipment at a scale sufficient for a mine taking out 3,000 tons of coal a day. Ever since its opening, visitors have been drawn to the *Coal Mine*'s enormous (three-story-high) head frame and startled by its sharp whistle as each group descends into the vertical shaft. Over the decades, as millions of visitors have entered this subterranean world, it has remained one of the Museum's most popular exhibits.

The *Coal Mine* represented a bold triumph; it blended technical knowhow with an unmistakable knack for showmanship. Such an exhibit – recounting the saga of bituminous coal – might have looked like an unglamourous idea when it was first proposed in the late 1920s. But through a process of careful planning, and with the addition of several inspired touches, the *Coal Mine* developed into something that would later be called an "icon" of the Museum, one of those enduring features that continue to draw streams of visitors, even after being on view for decades. The *Coal Mine* not only demonstrates a lively and exciting industry, it represents an impressive, oversized experience that looms large in the memories of generations of visitors.

Energy

This electrostatic generator, or "static machine," was made by James Wimshurst in 1884.

The idea for Chicago's *Coal Mine* came from a similar, smaller exhibit that the Museum's first director, Waldemar Kaempffert, admired at the Deutsches Museum in Munich. The founder of the Munich museum, Oskar von Miller, having moved his own institution into a new complex in 1925, wisely advised Kaempffert that such an installation was better designed before a new building was finished rather than afterward. He urged Kaempffert to work out the Museum's contents in detail before committing to a particular architectural scheme: if he wanted a coal mine, he should plan it right away.

Mining remained uppermost in Kaempffert's mind for other reasons as well. "Nothing has changed the world the way mining did," he repeated when he spoke to different groups about his new institution. Modern factories at that time depended almost entirely on coal as fuel. Coal, along with other minerals brought to the surface by miners, represented an essential raw material for the Industrial Revolution.

One of the first curators Kaempffert hired for the Museum was a geological engineer, Dr. James Van Pelt, who quickly began work on a mining exhibit. Van Pelt devised elaborate plans for a realistic mine, and in 1930 he discussed his ideas, still in the formative stages, on a local Chicago radio program. At that early date, Van Pelt envisioned a multipurpose exhibit with a twisting tunnel, first demonstrating gold mining, then copper, and ending with an expansive coal operation. Additional exhibits would deal with iron ore, smelting, steel making, and related processes.

Displays such as these were entirely fitting for a museum of industry, Van Pelt said. Mining might not seem to be a profession for visionaries, but it provided indispensable sources of energy required by the Machine Age, and the promise of mining for precious metals had helped drive America's expansion West. As the curator continued, "The mining engineer has always pushed out into the wilderness beyond the frontiers, has conquered the forces of nature against almost hopeless odds, and has brought back to civilization the gold and silver, the iron and copper, the coal and petroleum without which modern civilization could not survive for a single day."

48

PRECEDING PAGES
The Solar Fountain, which is a part of the *Energy Lab* exhibit, is powered by solar panels on the Museum's roof.

OPPOSITE
This complex, colorful web of pipes and boilers is a section of the infrastructure required to heat and cool the Museum's 750,000 square feet.

The *Coal Mine*, when it opened with the Museum in 1933, used equipment from a defunct mine in southern Illinois. Many things have changed at the Museum over the years, but the *Coal Mine* remains one of its most memorable and important "icons."

There had been moments when the *Coal Mine,* like the Museum itself, had seemed too large, too complicated, ever to be realized. After Kaempffert's resignation, financial troubles nearly brought work to a halt, and the gold- and copper-mining exhibits were set aside. Still, the founders had pressed ahead with the *Coal Mine,* for several reasons. One was its aptness as a starting point for telling the story of the modern industry. Perhaps equally important was its size, deemed appropriate for an institution envisioned as large and grand as industrial technology itself. Curiously in this regard, another early plan for the Museum was a one-tenth-scale re-creation of Niagara Falls, intended to demonstrate the generation of hydroelectric power. It would have featured the roaring sound of the true Falls along with special atomizers to create realistic mist. Curators hoped it might rival Chicago's Buckingham Fountain as an attraction.

Visitors descend to the basement of
the Museum and become immersed
in a realistic re-creation of a working
coal mine.

ENERGY

A mechanical hoist, such as this one in the *Coal Mine*, lowers miners into the pit and raises coal out of it. The diameter of the large cylinder exceeds 12 feet.

Such visions of the still-unopened Museum were very much on the mind of Kaempffert's successor, Otto Kreusser, formerly chief engineer of the General Motors Testing Ground in Michigan. By the time Kreusser arrived, the Niagara Falls exhibit had proven unworkable, but the new director made certain that the *Coal Mine* became a reality. Just weeks after assuming his post in Chicago, Kreusser made several trips throughout the Midwest to familiarize himself with what real mines actually looked like. During his travels, Kreusser found a coal operation in Johnston City, Illinois, recently shut down because of the Depression. Inquiring if the equipment was for sale, the director learned that it could all be taken away for the bargain-basement price of $10,000.

Buying a head frame was one thing, getting it into the Museum was another. Transporting the new acquisition to Chicago required an oversize flatbed truck and resourceful haulers and movers, who, at the end of their journey, had to maneuver the rigid 60-foot structure through the city's streets and finally into the Museum building. Like so many other events surrounding the new institution, this logistical feat attracted considerable newspaper attention, which helped make the *Coal Mine* familiar to many Chicagoans before it had even opened.

53

The *Coal Mine* became a must-see attraction for many as soon as it opened to the public, in the summer of 1933. Visitors rode down an elevator with stage curtains on either side that made the descent to the basement feel like a 3,000-foot drop. A chill draft toward the bottom added another touch of authenticity. Down below, the walls of the exhibit were built from plaster casts made in actual mines, and the timber supports holding up low ceilings were as realistic as possible. Visitors could also see the caged canaries, sensitive to changes in the atmosphere, which were used to give miners warning of methane gas leaks in the tunnels. Kreusser went so far as to have a kind of perfume devised to re-create the damp, musty smell of a true coal mine, and completing the illusion were a number of actual (retired) miners, operating the equipment with an easy professional familiarity.

Among the other early exhibits related to the Energy theme, many came about as a result of the Museum's cooperation with Chicago's second great world's fair, A Century of Progress. While the Museum and the fair were separate enterprises, they developed a close relationship as both labored mightily to open in 1933. The two projects were born of much the same spirit – A Century of Progress was devised, also by Chicago's business elite, to explore the impact of industrial technology on American life. The fair became a remarkable success as millions of visitors gazed into the technological future, and a more prosperous one at that. Like the Museum, the fair chronicled undeniable progress in transportation, manufacturing, and other sectors of the nation's industry.

Close ties naturally developed between the fair and the Museum, although the relationship encountered some stormy times in the early stages. The founders of the Museum were justifiably concerned that the fair, conceived well after their own plans had been announced, was appropriating many of their original ideas. In fact, fair organizers, including the banker Rufus Dawes and his brother Charles Gates Dawes, formerly vice president of the United States, issued statements describing A Century of Progress as "the dramatization of the progress of civilization." This sounded suspiciously similar to the way the Museum had already articulated its own mission. When fair organizers announced that its purpose was to "trace the technical ascent of man," people at the Museum recognized those words as their own.

Earth Trek, an exploration of oil and natural gas production, begins with primeval times when mastodons roamed the earth and the planet's great mineral deposits were being formed.

Ultimately, A Century of Progress and the Museum struck a formal agreement to cooperate in several mutually beneficial ways. A portion of this pact provided that the Museum's workshop, which already employed more than fifty designers and craftsmen, would conceive and build hundreds of exhibits and scientific models for the fair's Hall of Science. Many of those models would later go on permanent display at the Museum. In return for this service, the Museum would receive payment for the cost of labor – much needed at that point – and also receive a share of the fair's profits.

Many of the Museum's most successful early exhibits about energy and physics came out of this agreement. These ranged from the cross-section of a steam engine to a fully working electrostatic machine. Other devices were created to illustrate electromagnetism, with push buttons that activated electric motors and radio sets, and even demonstrated the principle of the X-ray. Indeed, the Museum's model shop was nothing if not ambitious. There was even talk at the outset of this project of "a model that will explain to a child just what Einstein's theory really means," according to one news report, though that effort was apparently unsuccessful.

The Museum's stairwells provide perfect opportunities for displaying its unusual artifacts, such as the Foucault Pendulum and a dramatic version of the periodic table.

Es 99
Einsteinium

Cf 98
Californium

Fm 100
~~rnium~~

Bk 97
Berkelium

Cm 96
Curium

Une 109
Unnilenium

Uno 108
Unniloctium

Uns 107
Unnilseptium

Une 109
Unnilenium

Live demonstrations bring activity, personality, and drama to the laws of science. In the early years of the Museum, the behavior of gases was regarded as the stuff of good theater.

As these and other Energy-related exhibits at the Museum evolved, they taught visitors of all ages the lessons of science and technology fundamental to life in the twentieth century. At the same time, curators and exhibit managers at the Museum were also learning – in their case, new ways to transmit information to the public. Among many lessons learned by the Museum, one was that relatively simple demonstrations could often successfully explain complicated principles. Another was that nothing held visitors' attention quite like sheer activity, whether in the form of wheels turning, lights flashing, or, particularly, an individual conducting an experiment.

Such insights were increasingly incorporated into the Museum's programs. By 1951, many were skillfully combined in a memorable exhibit on the subject of electrical energy called *Electric Theater*, sponsored by Commonwealth Edison. *Electric Theater* consisted of many participatory exhibits, such as a bicycle that generated electricity. It also featured a stage show that was uncommonly successful at getting visitors to think about technology. "It was set up to make people feel good about electricity," explained Herman Serieka, originally a salesman for the electric company who became master of ceremonies for this entertaining and educational program.

In recent years, a balloon, a Bunsen burner, and an animated demonstrator can create an engaging environment for visitors to learn the laws of science.

One of the first demonstrations of *Electric Theater* involved the universal childhood fascination with the firefly. "People believe that if we could produce light the way a fire-fly produces light," said Serieka, "we should have great quantities of light at very low cost." He then mixed the chemicals that scientists knew made fireflies light up, poured them into a vial, and held it up to show a dull glow. This was impressive, audience members might have thought, until Serieka told them that light produced this way would cost 25 million times more than light produced with energy from the utility company.

The electromagnetic spectrum was also given a leading role in the *Electric Theater* performance. Serieka would not only describe the abstract concepts of ultraviolet, infrared, and other kinds of rays, but also show how certain powders glowed when exposed to ultraviolet rays; it was the concept behind the relatively new technology of fluorescent lighting. Serieka also used infrared light to capture unlikely pictures on a phosphorescent screen. One such image showed the outline of a balloon at the instant it was popped. All of this comprised a brisk and entertaining show, and in the innocent days of cheap and risk-free energy, the message was as agreeable as Herman Serieka himself.

59

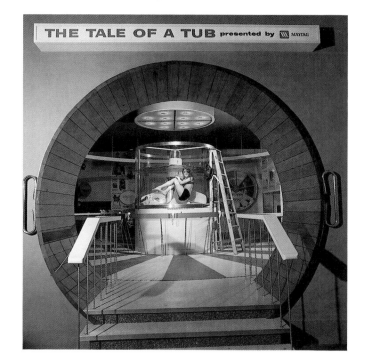

THE TALE OF A TUB presented by [MAYTAG]

In the 1960s this particular exhibit, *The Tale of a Tub,* took a humorous approach toward the mechanics of a larger-than-life-size washing machine.

Times were already changing, however. The Atomic Age had arrived, and the Museum of Science and Industry was naturally preparing itself to tell the complex story of nuclear energy. Over the decades, this story has changed and evolved, but from the beginning, exhibits on the subject have had a more subdued, and sometimes dramatic, tone.

Museum visitors had their first view of nuclear energy in 1948, in a presentation conceived by scientists at Argonne National Laboratory, one of the country's leading nuclear-research facilities. The items involved were relatively simple. They included a 54-pound piece of uranium ore inside a radiation-proof box equipped with a lever for visitors to press to feel its surprisingly heavy weight. A label explained that the half pound of fissionable material contained within this rock could produce enough energy to heat an average home for 40 to 50 years. The exhibit also had a section called "Hot Frogs," a small pond filled with frogs, some of which had been injected with minute trace amounts of radioactive material. As visitors directed a Geiger counter over the frogs, the "hot" ones triggered a buzzer and flashing light. The exhibit – its relative naïveté suggesting how new and unfamiliar the nuclear era still was – provided visitors with an idea of what nuclear medicine and radioactive isotopes could do.

Argonne Laboratory, under the Atomic Energy Commission and later the Department of Energy, maintained a close relationship with the Museum of Science and Industry for years. And as exhibits sponsored by the lab changed, their subjects reflected many critical and sometimes hotly debated issues connected to nuclear science.

A visitor walking through an oversize natural gas pipeline experiences a light show while listening to information regarding the transport of gas energy.

In the Grainger Hall of Basic Science, a visitor examines a two-dimensional model illustrating the earth's gravitational pull, which holds objects in a circular path.

In 1956, Argonne scientists assembled a major exhibit entitled *Atoms for Peace,* which opened first at a conference in Switzerland and shortly thereafter was brought to the Museum of Science and Industry. *Atoms for Peace* featured detailed models of many types of nuclear powerplants that were still in the design stage at the time. These were accompanied by explanations of America's fledgling program to get such facilities actually built and producing energy.

Scientists at Argonne readily admitted that only a small percentage of visitors to the Museum spent much time with their exhibits, but they believed that important ideas were getting through nonetheless. Museum officials also felt that there was real value in nuclear-science programs, which encouraged nonscientists to look into the major scientific issues of the day. "I don't think there's much to worry about at present," said Robert Adler, a student at Austin High School, in an interview by the *Chicago Sun-Times* during this period. Adler had just attended a Museum seminar on the many uses of atomic energy. "But we mustn't overlook the fact that this business could develop into something that could destroy the whole earth," he concluded.

As time passed, however, controversy over nuclear energy heated up, with the scientific community growing polarized about the goals of research, and the public's perception changing as well. These circumstances made nuclear-related programs at the Museum increasingly problematic. Although exhibits continued to explore various aspects of nuclear energy, there was definite concern about the risk of controversy. While a postwar exhibit on the medical aspects of atomic energy showed photos of the nuclear explosion at Hiroshima, the subject was considered out of step with the times at the Museum. That exhibit was short-lived and the theme was not repeated.

The Grainger Hall of Basic Science addresses fundamental subjects such as biology, chemistry, physics, and mathematics.

63

Nuclear science continued to play a role in the Museum in the 1980s and 1990s. The objective of these exhibits, as always, was the clear explanation of technology for young people and adults. Yet nuclear energy by this time evoked loud and often polarized debate. For this reason, exhibits on this subject now require increased sensitivity to, if not a focus on, delicate political issues.

This was evident in the renovation of an exhibit called *Energy Lab* in 1993 and a new section designed to illustrate the many steps involved in the production of nuclear energy. Like many exhibits at the Museum, this one was large and three-dimensional, featuring an interactive Geiger counter along with full-scale devices used to mine uranium and safely dispose of spent fuel rods. The exhibit was successful in explaining a complex process.

Nevertheless, the exhibit also reflected the difficulty of addressing nuclear issues. When it opened, the story it told raised concerns on both sides. People with antinuclear views found the straightforward approach of the exhibit to be distinctly in favor of the technology. Those on the other side were concerned mostly because of a video display that explained in vivid terms the risks of nuclear energy, highlighted by the disasters at Three Mile Island and Chernobyl.

Different reactions in the same exhibit underlined the difficulty of examining highly politicized subjects in this or any other museum. Ideally, the clear presentation of scientific fact ought to clarify issues and advance useful debate. But in the midst of sharp controversy, the gray areas of the most difficult issues can be lost despite the pursuit of hard scientific fact. This represents an age-old struggle at the Museum and a challenge for the future.

The Museum of Science and Industry seeks to demonstrate that technology at its best evolves in the service of human needs and ends, even in its theoretical and developmental stages. The exhibit called *Superconductivity,* for example, mounted for six months in 1988, focused on the seemingly abstract principle that electricity performs with remarkable efficiency at temperatures as low as absolute zero. Known since 1911, this concept took on new promise in 1986 when IBM research personnel in Switzerland demonstrated that superconductivity could be achieved at higher temperatures than previously thought. With newly developed ceramic materials, superconducting efficiency could be achieved well above absolute zero, at temperatures far easier and cheaper to produce.

There was something exhilarating about this news, beyond the excitement normally caused by discoveries in science. In large part this was because the advance foreshadowed potentially dramatic results. It was believed that electric motors of untold power, and microprocessors of unimaginable speed, might now be possible. These applications depended upon several practical refinements, however, and scientists at Argonne, a leader in superconductivity research, believed that success would come from private industry's getting behind the technology and pushing it toward economic feasibility.

Generating enthusiasm was very much Argonne's motive in helping the Museum develop a lively exhibit. The laboratory had already been doing demonstrations for several years in venues ranging from the Department of Energy in Washington to local chambers of commerce. With the benefit of this experience, the Museum's *Superconductivity* exhibit achieved considerable drama when a live demonstrator poured liquid nitrogen onto the coils of small electromagnets and produced enough power to levitate a ceramic disk the size of a hockey puck. This impressive sight aroused the curiosity of many visitors, as expected, and many went further into the exhibit, which delved deeper into the subject through illustrations and videos.

Most spectacular among applications shown in *Superconductivity* was a kind of railroad, in this case a futuristic monorail levitated by superconducting electromagnets. A video of a Japanese prototype left visitors with a vivid idea of the technology's power. Curiously, the vision of this advanced monorail was shown not far from some of the oldest and most familiar exhibits of the Museum: its old railroad engines. It seemed like mere coincidence, but one not lost on the most attentive visitors, nor on creative exhibit designers.

Superconductivity was a brief exhibit, but it demonstrated what the Museum of Science and Industry was determined to accomplish. It sought to explore one of the newest areas in energy research at the time. It also reached into many other fields – physics, material science, engineering, and computer technology – and showed how all have a role in superconductivity's development. *Superconductivity* vividly demonstrated how a fresh application of the basic laws of electromagnetism may soon lead to new kinds of tools used by everyone, moving its future development from the confines of the research laboratory and into the arena of public discussion.

Most of all, *Superconductivity* pointed to the critical importance of future research. "What is clear is that important work in this field will be done by people who are now in high school," said an Argonne scientist involved in the exhibit. This suggests the intriguing possibility that some future scientists, who will make key discoveries about superconductivity, may perhaps have first seen the technology with their parents and friends while on a visit to the Museum of Science and Industry.

65

In January 1941, the Museum of Science and Industry celebrated an elaborate gala – the first of many in the long tenure of Major Lenox R. Lohr as its president. It marked the opening of the *Museum & Santa Fe Railroad,* the largest model railroad in the world. Planning for this expansive exhibit had begun well before "the Major," as he was always called, took the controls of the Museum, but the event was an appropriate way for the Lohr years to begin.

Major Lohr was recruited by trustees in 1940. In his 28 years as the Museum's powerful chief executive, the Major would demonstrate a wide spectrum of talents, but the most urgent imperative when he arrived was nothing less than saving the institution from collapse. Before his arrival, the Museum had not yet recovered from the effects of the Great Depression. With its vast interior still incomplete, trustees had wondered whether Dr. Philip Fox, the astronomer who succeeded Otto Kreusser as director, possessed the practical skills to bring to fruition the Museum's early promise.

When approached to head the Museum, Lohr was president of the National Broadcasting Company in New York. He was no stranger to Chicago, however, having been general manager of A Century of Progress, still vividly remembered as one of Chicago's most successful enterprises. Indeed, the Major cut a commanding figure, a no-nonsense former military man who also possessed the deft touch of a showman. Throughout his career, he had set many ambitious goals and had achieved them. The trustees hoped he could work his magic on the Museum of Science and Industry.

Transportation

This section of a 727 engine displays a marvelous mechanical symmetry.

Certainly, the new model railroad provided an auspicious start for the Major, an exhibit very much in the "Lohrian" (that is to say grandiose) mold. Conceived and built by the leading model railroader in the country, Minton Cronkhite, the layout covered 3,000 square feet, with 350 feet of main track (1,000 feet altogether, including sidings and switching systems). Model railroading was in its infancy at the time, but Cronkhite's work was striking for its attention to detail. Locomotives and rolling stock were handmade in his own shops and cast in his own "Q" scale, similar to the standard "O" but considered more realistic by the hobby's leading experts.

The *Museum & Santa Fe* quickly became famous, drawing praise not only from the railroad press, as might have been expected, but also from newspapers and magazines around the country and abroad. Besides fine engines and cars, it featured an elaborate signal system, with red, yellow, and green lights modeled closely after actual railroads. It was controlled from a Centralized Traffic Control (CTC) Board made by the Union Switch & Signal Company, supplier to many real switchyards. The layout was also equipped with scale models of factories, such as a locomotive works, an oil refinery, a cement plant, and a grain elevator, each with moving parts of its own.

In its attention to realistic detail, the *Museum & Santa Fe* was a remarkable piece of craftsmanship, demonstrating great ingenuity. But the overall effect – when visitors walked upstairs to the balcony overhead and saw the railroad as a whole – was even more impressive. Its trains moved through a varied terrain of pine forest, desert, and even a convincing rendering of the Grand Canyon. At a time when most model railroads were skeletal and crude, this one set a new standard of sophistication. And its image of industrial harmony conveyed a message about the role of the railroad in American life, a vital transportation link binding together a nation of great beauty and technological might.

As the Lohr years at the Museum began, the power of American industry emerged as the dominant theme of the Museum of Science and Industry. As at A Century of Progress, this would require the closest cooperation with private enterprise. With a sense of firm resolve, Lohr began his tenure at the Museum with a jolt, firing most of the curators and precipitating a furious but short-lived tempest in the scholarly community. He did this largely because he believed that most of them were unable to forge fruitful relationships with industry. Allying the Museum with business required a different mentality, giving greater attention to public relations and handling exhibits with more fanfare.

In the case of the model railroad, this began with the grand formal luncheon to honor the exhibit's sponsor, the Atchison, Topeka & Santa Fe Railway Company, with its executives and other railroad officials from around the country in attendance. The event was even broadcast on NBC radio. When Santa Fe president Edward J. Engel rose to speak at the luncheon, he addressed not just the assembled guests, but a nationwide broadcast audience.

It was the kind of public opportunity that business leaders coveted. Engel spoke of America's position in railroading, and the railroads' indispensable role in the expanding American economy. The Major also spoke, thanking Engel and his company for the lavish new exhibit that he said "vividly demonstrates the Museum's theme – the partnership of science and industry." Lohr went on to talk about the model railroad as a teaching tool for children and adults alike, giving a sense of the nation as an interconnected network of industry and technology. As always, Lohr emphasized the broad lessons. "The important thing is not to be distracted by the complexities of intricate patterns, but to endeavor to understand the basic forces that form them," he said.

Though the idea of railroading was given a new drama by the *Museum & Santa Fe,* trains had been a part of the Museum's exhibits from the beginning. Among the earliest contributions to the Museum were a number of antique locomotives from the storage houses of the Illinois Central Railroad. One of these, an 1834-vintage relic called the *Mississippi,* came with a marvelous story that spoke volumes about America's railroading past, and even provided some early insight into the Museum itself.

One of the oldest locomotives in the country, the *Mississippi* represented an intriguing challenge for the early curators who sought to unravel its past and hoped eventually to restore its original appearance. It was known that this locomotive had been on display in the Transportation Building at the World's Columbian Exposition in 1893. Before that, it had operated in western Mississippi for virtually all of its working life. But the locomotive's origins remained vague, until the Museum's curator of transportation and communications, S. C. GilFillan, set out to find them. His research showed that the engine had been built in England in the shops of Braithwaite, Milner & Company in 1834, though GilFillan, hoping that the locomotive might have been of American manufacture, was reluctant at first to accept that finding.

69

English manufacture was proven, but the *Mississippi* had a true American story to tell. After it was built, the locomotive was immediately shipped to America, then floated down the Ohio and Mississippi rivers to Natchez. It was put in service on the Natchez & Hamburg Railroad, one of the earliest rail companies in the South. In the 1860s, the small steam engine saw action in the Civil War as the Confederate army used it during the siege of Vicksburg. It was later commandeered by the Union army, then, after the war, it was scuttled in mud by an inattentive engineer. During the 1870s, the *Mississippi* was found, cleaned, and brought back to working order, then saw service for another decade or two in a gravel operation in Brookhaven, Mississippi.

GilFillan and others at the Museum wanted to restore this historic locomotive to its original state, but like many projects in the early years, this one had to be put off. Delay was partly a matter of priorities, but also reflected continued uncertainty about the engine's original design. "It is well," wrote one researcher in 1928, "even in a collection of antique locomotives, to have at least one locomotive, about which a mystery hovers." The *Mississippi* became known as "our Mystery Locomotive."

Much later, in 1965, the *Mississippi* was indeed faithfully restored, and today it occupies a permanent place not far from the model railroad, both of which remain venerable attractions of the Museum's modern Transportation Zone.

When Major Lohr arrived at the Museum in 1940, he was less interested in the quaint sense of "mystery" surrounding an antique locomotive than in the larger drama of modern industry it suggested. He wanted to mount displays that represented the workings of vast and powerful forces.

"There is intense drama in the functioning of industry," the Major said (in one of the many tape recordings he made while musing alone in his office after-hours). "But it needs pointing up – ballyhoo if you like – to focus public attention on it."

Scholarship alone would never satisfy his plans. "The interpretation of the part that industry must play in building the American Way of Life," he said, "is a definite part of the

Museum philosophy and method of public display." He was certain that major corporations would be eager to participate in this endeavor: "The Museum offers a medium through which industry can combat the antagonism toward capitalistic structures."

An unabashed Americanism was always just beneath the surface of what the Major said and wrote. And while the exigencies of World War II distracted private industry from the Museum of Science and Industry for several years, Lohr set about fostering an institution that projected a kind of patriotism in everything it did. "In these days of world change," he said, "it becomes increasingly important that the fundamentals of American democracy be portrayed."

As the war limited the ability of companies to bring sponsored exhibits into the Museum, the ever-resourceful Major made the best of hard times, mounting military-related displays and even turning over some of the galleries to the armed services for use in basic scientific training.

Lohr's wartime programs at the Museum were highly publicized. Most enduring was the inauguration of *Christmas Around the World.* Beginning in 1941, this annual festival brought many ethnic groups to the Museum in a harmonious celebration of the nation's cultural diversity. It was one of many exhibits and events of this period that associated the Museum with honored American values – and not so incidentally as a place where American industry would be eager to have its presence felt.

As the war wound down, the Major brought corporations in and did so in big ways. The *Chicago Tribune,* for example, installed a large printing press on the Museum's premises and even printed a portion of its Sunday paper there so that the public could see its operation. International Harvester displayed historical reapers as well as giant tractors. The Aluminum Company of America installed an exhibit that illustrated many uses of the relatively novel metal – even as a structural material in a realistic section of a full-size house. Nevertheless, Lohr was careful to mute any overt commercial message that might be found in these exhibits. Visitors would be more impressed, he insisted, by the accurate demonstration of technology itself.

71

The Major's feel for impressing and even dazzling visitors paid off in many ways. By the middle 1940s, the Museum had become Chicago's most popular cultural institution, with an annual attendance of a million and a half visitors. The Lohr years were also notable for establishing a number of long-lived "icons" of the Museum. One icon, created somewhat later in Lohr's tenure, was the *Pioneer Zephyr*, which came courtesy of the Chicago Burlington & Quincy Railroad. This streamlined, stainless-steel passenger train had represented an important advance in railroad technology when it was introduced to the public in 1933. Features such as its new diesel engines and low center of gravity made it the fastest thing on tracks, and it was copied by other railroads around the world.

ABOVE

At the turn of the century, the "999" was the largest and most powerful locomotive on the tracks.

RIGHT

72

The *Pioneer Zephyr*, the original "streamliner" of the 1930s, set records for speed and offered the latest in comfort when it was introduced at the height of the railroad era.

A visitor enjoys the chance to explore the operating controls of one of the Museum's trains.

By 1960, however, the *Pioneer Zephyr* was ready to be retired, and the Museum was viewed as an appropriate resting place. Certainly, the *Zephyr* deserved an honored place in transportation history as a high-water mark of rail travel that was as luxurious as it was efficient. At the same time, the retirement of the *Pioneer Zephyr* represented a sad downturn in the fortunes of the passenger railroads, a great industry in decline while airports and interstate highways were being built – with heavy federal subsidy – at a frenzied pace. A complex symbol of America's shift from past to present, the *Zephyr* quickly became an object of fascination for visitors to the Museum.

Today, the *Pioneer Zephyr,* restored to its original glory by a refurbishing completed in 1997, remains an impressive piece of engineering. A fine example of the "streamlining" so popular in the 1930s, it still appears remarkably forward-looking. Its design elegance and its speed capability are anything but antiquated, even compared to modern jet planes (which, the truth be told, rarely outpace good passenger-train service on many shorter routes). Museum visitors who walk through the *Zephyr* often ask why something that worked so well for so long was largely abandoned. It is a question that can tell us a great deal about the larger dynamics of innovation, and about the mission of the Museum to preserve and explain the history of technological change.

73

As a place designed to capture the spirit of technology, the Museum of Science and Industry is especially proud of its automobile collection, which features a range of antique and classic cars, along with some futuristic ones. Bringing these examples together was another significant accomplishment of Major Lohr, an early collector of automobiles in the era before they were widely coveted or prohibitively expensive. The Major's passion for old cars, like his vision of the Museum as a whole, revealed both the history and "romance" of machines.

Indeed, Lohr's own collection of autos – many of which now belong to the Museum – demonstrated a very personal touch. While the Museum of Science and Industry generally focuses its attention on the latest technology, the Major found in historical cars a crucial bridge between the feelings and values of human beings and the new, metallic world of twentieth-century machines. In autos, he recognized something that was growing in American society at the time – a kind of love affair between people and technology, especially technology that gave them new freedom.

Not long after he became president of the Museum, the Major's own affection for automobiles led him to stage a reenactment on the fiftieth anniversary of a milestone of automotive history: the 1895 *Times-Herald* Race, the earliest auto race in the United States. Lohr later described this historic event in a lecture he delivered before the Newcomen Society, a gathering of England's leading figures of technology and engineering. In his remarks, he recounted the sometimes comical race which started and finished outside the building that would be the Museum. He described how Frank Duryea, one of America's automotive pioneers, won the 54-mile event in something over ten hours.

Mostly, Lohr's speech marveled at the diversity of approaches to automotive engineering that appeared on that day in Chicago. There were gasoline and steam engines, steering wheels and tillers. This led to Lohr's major point. It was that the familiar automobile of postwar America, with internal combustion and rear-wheel drive, may have evolved as the standard design, but there was still room for other ideas.

"Instead of our cars being as much alike as two peas in a pod, perhaps we can once again revel in a choice of front-wheel drive, rear engines, turbines, jet or atomic propulsion," he said. "Perhaps once again we may meet old friends like steamers and electrics."

Today's automotive exhibits at the Museum would please Major Lohr. They feature many fine historic specimens, showing something of the technology's evolution and the entirely human choices made along the way. Some demonstrate how much the earliest auto makers looked to the trustworthy buggy when designing the new "horseless" carriages. The auto exhibits also include an old favorite at the Museum, *Yesterday's Main Street,* constructed in the late 1940s. Although Main Street, replicating a stretch of an old Chicago thoroughfare from 1910, constituted an undeniable bit of nostalgia, it also made the illuminating point that cars and cobbled business streets had been designed very much for one another.

Other lessons from the automobile collection are particular to varied models manufactured and driven at various points in history. Among early treasures of the Museum, its 1904 "curved-dash" Olds represents one of the first mass-produced models in America, lovingly engineered, and with touches of the rakish charm to which car makers have often aspired. A Ford Model-T shows a quite different attitude that was also at work in the infant industry – and a set of decisions that made Henry Ford one of the great magnates of the twentieth century. The Model-T, entirely more practical, stands stripped of almost all unnecessary expense. It bears witness to Ford's ambition to put a car in every garage, and his ironic claim that a Ford automobile was available in every color – as long as it was black.

Yesterday's Main Street is a nostalgic return to an early American city street, featuring some of the nation's first automobiles.

75

As our century progressed, of course, the great attraction of automobiles was that they satisfied a taste for finery as well as the simple need for transportation. And as the Museum's collection developed, mostly in the 1950s, it gravitated to the luxurious side of the technology as well. Among the Museum's classic cars, many handmade works of automotive art reflect the ambition not to cut expenses, but to add as much as possible.

In this regard, the Museum's 1929 Rolls-Royce is not only a marvelous thing to behold, but also comes with an evocative bit of social history. As the property of the William McCormick Blair family, this Rolls spent years touring the continental United States, and logged miles in all 48 states, the story goes, before retiring to its present home. Now a minor icon of the Museum, it seems to symbolize the marriage of impeccable engineering and apparently limitless wealth.

Like other forms of transportation, aviation has long played an important role at the Museum. Since its earliest years, the Museum has acquired a number of full-size airplanes, from primitive biplanes to the swift Stuka and Spitfire of World War II vintage. Airplanes installed inside the Museum have always kept visitors riveted. In the early years, they were amazing new "flying machines"; as time has transformed them into antiques, they have helped to illustrate the almost unbelievable progress aviation has made in little more than a single lifetime.

Despite the Museum's familiarity with airplane exhibits, United Airlines' offer of a full-size 727 airliner, about to be taken out of service, was no routine acquisition. The eventual exhibit, called *Take Flight,* was the result of an initial agreement between Dr. Kahn, president of the Museum, and Stephen Wolfe, chairman of United Airlines. But well before its 1994 opening the exhibit staff took a hard look not just at the enormous artifact, but at the Museum's ability to exhibit and interpret it.

77

Take Flight explores the science of
aeronautics with a variety of advanced
interactive exhibits. The jetliner hang-
ing from the balcony quickly grabs
the attention of youngsters and adults
alike.

Ultimately, *Take Flight* was as large and unwieldy an endeavor as anything the Museum had ever undertaken. It was three arduous years in the making, but in the end it became a popular and artistic success. The exhibit was the result of a complex collaboration – not only with the airline and with Boeing, the plane's manufacturer, but with the many others who helped devise a way to bring a modern jetliner indoors and carve from it a compelling and superbly educational artifact.

The process of designing *Take Flight* was an immensely detailed undertaking, but as the exhibit was actually assembled, the process took on the aura of an epic. Shortly after the Museum and the airline came to an agreement, for example, an event was scheduled at Meigs Field, where the jet would come in for its final landing. The old downtown airport was unaccustomed to a plane of such size, and the landing – something of a feat on the modest runway – created a stir all along Chicago's lakefront. The juxtaposition of old and new gave the people assembled on the tarmac that day a chance to think a little more deeply about a technology that had become almost commonplace in American life – which was also the objective of the exhibit that Museum officials had in mind.

The epic continued as the jet was floated by barge to an empty field in nearby Indiana. A year later, the 727 was finally ready to be taken to the Museum, floated back to Chicago, pulled up the beach, and towed across the parking lot in an effort that recalled the process of getting the Museum's famous *U-505* submarine over a similar distance just 40 years before. Lake Shore Drive had to be closed, and thousands turned out to witness the giant airplane's transit.

The 727 remained behind the Museum for some months where it was a sometimes startling sight for commuters driving by. Meanwhile, engineers made plans to get it indoors and installed as the centerpiece of what had already become one of the most anticipated exhibits in the Museum in years.

"It was a winning subject from the beginning," said one of the exhibit designers. "We were talking about a basic question: Why do things fly?" Still, providing detailed answers while also sustaining the visitor's curiosity remained a major challenge. After much discussion, the designers made the first of many important decisions: to make the jetliner appear to be in flight.

79

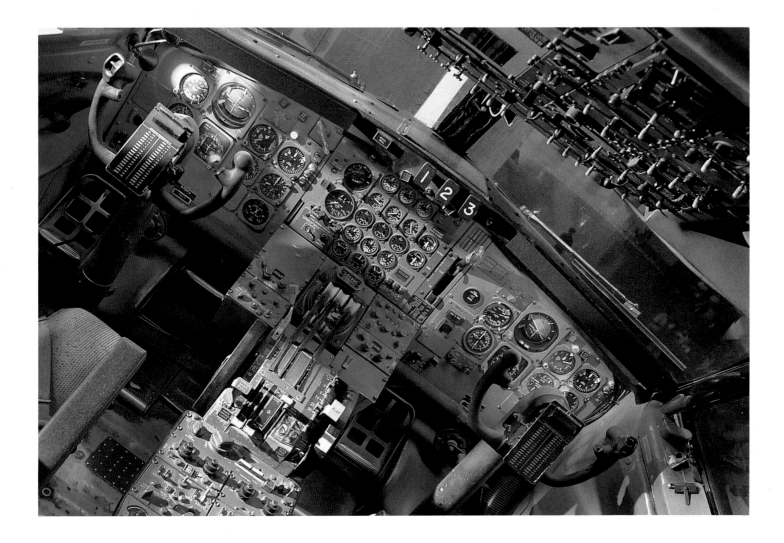

Once inside the 727, the visitor
can go to the cockpit to study the
complex instrumentation a pilot
must master.

80

To accomplish this, they sheered off one wing and suspended the plane lengthways along the balcony, no small feat of engineering. Then they opened the sides of the plane and placed inside a variety of interactive devices illustrating the science and technology of flight. Outside, they designed a dramatic illusion of the 727 landing, with lights flashing, landing gear in motion, and music playing on loudspeakers in a performance that was repeated several times a day. In broad outline, *Take Flight* resembled other major exhibits at the Museum of Science and Industry. It represented a familiar image taken out of its normal environment, its drama heightened in a way to help teach its hidden secrets.

The drama was the easy part, of course. Conveying the fundamental physics of aviation was more difficult. For the most part, this was uncharted terrain, though the timeless lessons of motion, sound, and hands-on learning were prominent at every step. Still, *Take Flight*'s designers also drew on ambitious and even experimental teaching techniques to transmit complex dimensions of the subject. One set of interactives in the exhibit addresses the physics of aviation and the so-called "four forces of flight," weight, lift, drag, and thrust. Among these, a wind tunnel and a section of wing enable visitors to feel the lift that actually makes planes fly. Another device, a computer with touch screens, guides a visitor through the design of an airplane in a way that considers the "four forces." Other interactives demonstrate the workings of a gyroscope, essential to pilots in keeping a plane steady when the horizon has disappeared, and the techniques of navigation, using basic readings and instrumentation. These detailed presentations proved nearly as popular as the giant airplane itself and its light-and-sound performance.

The reasons for the success of *Take Flight* are not new. Its techniques hark back to the concepts of the great educator John Dewey, who was convinced that the body should be engaged as well as the brain, for learning to be truly memorable. These ideas were used in the earliest object-lessons imagined by curators at the Museum of Science and Industry. The ideas also guided the design of large-scale exhibits with awesome sights and impressive sounds. *Take Flight* also recalls the importance that Major Lohr assigned to automobiles, a technology that triggers many thoughts, emotions, and ultimately a range of new questions. *Take Flight* demonstrates the central role of a museum of technology – to focus most closely on machines common enough to be familiar, but complex enough to arouse curiosity. This exhibit, like so many at the Museum of Science and Industry, points to that delicate formula and applies it so that true learning might take place.

81

In 1957, the Soviet Union shocked the world by putting into orbit a tiny satellite called *Sputnik*. It was humanity's first venture into the fringes of outer space, and it was obvious that the feat required not simply political determination but also a high level of technical and scientific skill. Americans, sharply embarrassed by their failure to be the first into space, wondered whether they would ever catch up.

Sputnik made it clear that a concerted national effort would be required, beginning with a new emphasis on education. Few people growing up in the late 1950s and the 1960s have forgotten the dramatic push given to science training at the dawn of the Space Age. All across the country, from primary schools to the most advanced graduate programs, mathematics and the physical sciences were given the highest priority. Almost overnight, these subjects, sometimes regarded in the past as abstractions, became the focus of an intense national commitment. Although this level of resolve would not be sustained in the years to follow, hardly anything ever captured the American imagination quite like the idea of putting human beings into space.

The lessons of that era gave rise to a new focus on space exploration in the 1960s. The infinitely complex adventure of space travel gave a human face to science and technology, opening the imagination to challenging technical subjects, providing incentive to master what might otherwise seem daunting. Physics, mathematics, biology, and chemistry took on compelling new life as part of efforts to send human beings beyond our own planet. Abstract concepts of the solar system became real, and blackboard calculations, a matter of life and death.

Space and Defense

83

This breathtaking scene is from *Antarctica*, an Omnimax movie produced by the Museum.

The Museum's relationship with the National Aeronautics and Space Administration goes back to 1961, when NASA brought in an exhibit entitled *Men in Space.* Installed in the rotunda, it featured models of many early satellites then in orbit, dramatizing "man's first steps in the quest for greater knowledge of the Earth's environment," the exhibit explained. It also included a seven-story-high Scout rocket, erected before the front steps of the Museum.

Men in Space excited those already interested in rocket science. People not particularly drawn to the subject, it was later discovered, were often somewhat confused, in part because the exhibit consisted largely of unmanned orbiters despite its title *Men in Space.* "We were quick to learn that manned exploration had the real power for youngsters and adults," said Daniel M. MacMaster, then director and later president of the Museum of Science and Industry.

Space science needed a personal element to get its message across, and this realization led to a series of Saturday lectures at the Museum in 1961 and 1962 by a charismatic professor of physics from DePaul University, Dr. Daniel Q. Posin. Astronomy was Dr. Posin's area of expertise, but he spoke on a range of related subjects, including one lecture – entitled "Who Are the Martians?" – on the whole question of extraterrestrial life. Other celestial bodies, too, seemed within grasp as Dr. Posin described them in the liveliest terms, explaining mathematical formulae one moment, and in the next wondering out loud whether the mists of Venus might not shroud primeval marshes where turtles lived. (Ultimately, he judged this unlikely.) Dr. Posin's lectures filled the Museum auditorium every Saturday, not only with youngsters but with surprising numbers of adults as well, anxious to find a way into the dense subject of astrophysics.

Soon, manned space travel became a reality. Following another Soviet first, the 1961 flight of the cosmonaut Yuri Gagarin, NASA's Mercury program put Alan Shepard in space and then John Glenn into orbit, circling the earth three times in February 1962. Rivalry with the Soviet Union had made space science a U.S. priority, but the long-awaited success of Glenn's flight made it a national passion.

After his triumphant flight, Glenn made a highly publicized visit to the Museum in 1963 to open a new exhibit on space exploration. His visit was carried live on television, and the astronaut used the occasion to deliver a message much like the Museum's own: "We will need more astronauts, scientists, and astronomers in this space age, and I urge the youth of our country to get the best education."

The drama of space science intensified over the next few years as the race to the moon hurtled to a finish. At the Museum, excitement reached a high pitch in early 1969 with the visit of the crew of *Apollo 8*. William Anders, Frank Borman, and James Lovell had made history only a month before with their Christmas Eve orbital flight around the moon – a feat never before accomplished. When they visited Chicago, the city was theirs: after a ticker tape parade down LaSalle Street, they were made honorary citizens.

Perhaps more than ever before, the *Apollo* crew made the space program a personal drama. Speaking in Chicago that day, Borman recited the same lines from Scripture that he had read out loud on Christmas Eve night as *Apollo 8* pulled into lunar orbit. On a lighter note, Lovell recounted his problems with a science project that he had attempted as a schoolboy in Milwaukee, trying to launch a model rocket. When he had called Chicago to buy the necessary chemicals, suppliers told him that compounds like potassium nitrate were available only by the carload.

Quite naturally, the visiting *Apollo* astronauts were also escorted to the Museum of Science and Industry, where they were greeted by crowds on the steps. Inside, they toured many exhibits, focusing particularly on the Hall of Communications, where they noted a miniature satellite transmitting an actual television signal. In another exhibit, where steel balls and a cone-like surface were used to illustrate the mathematics of orbital flight, the astronauts used the device as a visual aid to explain these principles to members of their entourage.

In 1971 the *Apollo 8* capsule was lifted above the caryatids to enter through the Museum's roof.

85

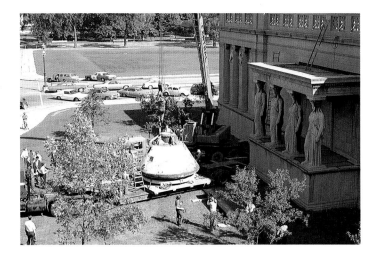

Since the *Apollo 8* capsule was too
wide to fit through any of the
Museum's doors, a hole was cut in
the roof of the East Pavilion, and
a crane lowered the craft carefully
into place.

SPACE AND DEFENSE

Several months after this visit, as the series of Apollo moon landings began, exhibits on space travel became regular events at the Museum. First came a number of special attractions, such as a heavily attended weekend exhibit of lunar rocks, and another with rare video footage from the moon. Shortly after these blockbusters, representatives of the Museum were invited to Silver Hill, Maryland, where the Smithsonian Institution maintained a warehouse full of priceless space-related artifacts that had not yet been put on exhibit. There, a member of the Museum exhibit staff spotted the *Apollo 8* capsule. The Smithsonian quickly agreed that the spacecraft of Anders, Borman, and Lovell should take up permanent residence in Chicago – a proposition that was easier said than done. When the capsule arrived, in 1971, the Museum was obliged to cut a hole in the building's roof in order to lower it, by crane, into its exhibit hall.

The *Apollo 8* crew has maintained a close relationship with the Museum, visiting frequently and lending many personal items from their flight, such as Borman's spacesuit, Lovell's flight manual, and even a bottle of brandy, carried aboard for Christmas Eve but never consumed.

After the Apollo flights ended in 1972, space travel seemed to lose some of its sparkle. NASA's next endeavors were focused more on technical experiments and less on stunning feats of human exploration. The Space Shuttle program, when it began in the 1970s, drew some interest back to the efforts of scientists, engineers, pilots, and others. But when space travel seemed to become something almost routine, even commonplace, public interest diminished once again.

Still, the Museum maintained a focus on space science and technology, and in the mid-1980s several events brought space travel back into the Museum's limelight. An important milestone was reached in 1986 with the opening of the Henry Crown Space Center. This project was conceived when members of the philanthropic Crown family met with Museum officials and asked then-president Victor Danilov for a "wish list" of new projects. A space pavilion was one of them, and the family quickly agreed that this would be appropriate, given their relationship with General Dynamics, a major space-industries contractor.

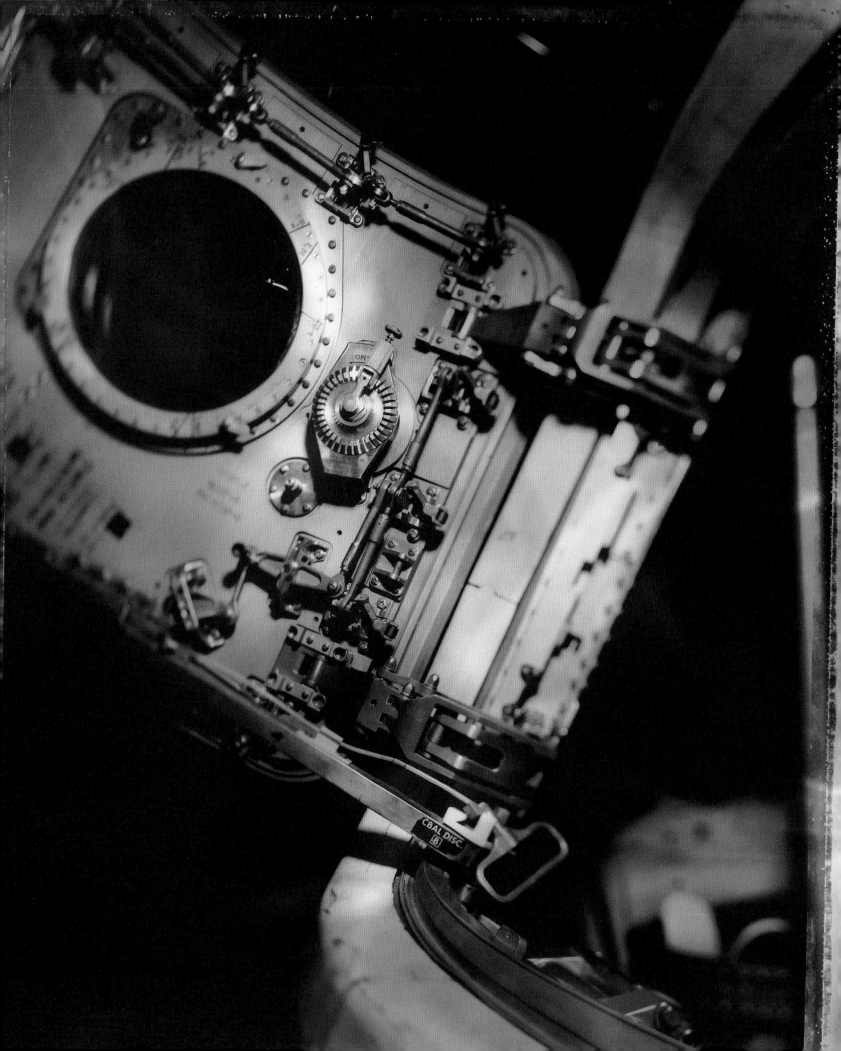

OPPOSITE

A detailed look at the door of the *Apollo 8* capsule reveals its complex engineering.

ABOVE

The exterior of the capsule was burned after its perilous re-entry into the earth's atmosphere.

RIGHT

Little room was provided for the astronauts inside the capsule.

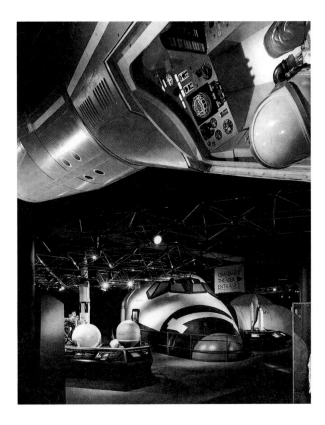

In the Henry Crown Space Center, the *Apollo 8* capsule joins a number of other space artifacts chronicling America's odyssey from the earliest satellites to the NASA Space Shuttle. Children as well as former astronauts come to visit the space capsules in the Center.

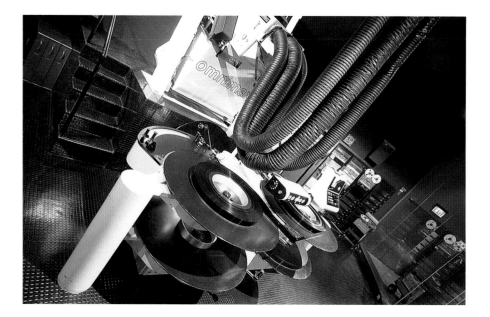

The Omnimax Theater provides the most lifelike film experience possible. Its projection system uses 15,000 watts of electricity to illuminate the projector and threads a three-and-a-half-mile-long line of film through the spools.

Construction of the Henry Crown Space Center also involved adding a related attraction to the Museum, the 400-seat Omnimax Theater. IMAX and Omnimax film technology – using film stock of enormous format with a massive screen – had been invented in the late 1960s and introduced at Expo '67, the Montreal world's fair. High-definition Omnimax images created a visual field like nothing then in existence; projected on curved screens, the images were astonishingly close-up and lifelike. They brought viewers into visceral contact with new and unknown worlds.

Omnimax re-created the sensations of air and space travel with a special vividness, and when the Henry Crown Space Center opened, its first Omnimax film was a joint production of NASA and the Smithsonian. *The Dream Is Alive* was shot by astronauts themselves, mostly on an early voyage of the Space Shuttle *Challenger*. This motion picture was dazzling beyond anything that most people had ever seen, depicting the weightless environment of the cabin and the crystal-clear panorama outside the spacecraft.

Something else brought record-breaking crowds to see *The Dream Is Alive*. In a poignant way, the film enabled the audience to pay homage to lost astronauts – the seven crew members who died when the *Challenger* exploded on takeoff in January 1986. Suddenly, the human element in space travel had been underscored by a tragic event, and the film, which featured astronauts who perished, carried significance that was unanticipated when the footage was shot. With the Space Shuttle program on hold after the *Challenger* disaster, *The Dream Is Alive* found an audience of nearly 500,000 during its seven-month Chicago run.

The theater's domed screen is 76 feet in diameter and is tilted 30 degrees to heighten the drama of the experience.

Subsequent big-screen productions went into other subjects, with great success. Filmmakers had discovered that Omnimax was suited not only to the vastness of space, but to terrestrial environments as well. This was very much the case with an important Omnimax film for which the Museum served as producer, *Antarctica,* which premiered in 1991.

Antarctica was a natural subject for Omnimax. The spacious beauty of the frozen continent projects well in the Omnimax format, and its scientific importance is of a similar impact. This became clear when Australian documentary filmmaker John Weiley approached the Museum for support of such a project. The result became a motion picture of large and quiet images, with scenes such as the silent "ballet" of emperor penguins in crystalline underwater ice caves. Here, the ability of Omnimax to fill the viewer's entire field of vision rivets attention as almost nothing else can. As in many of the best Omnimax films, words are kept to an elegant minimum while still conveying both a scientific story and the poetic essence of the place. Explorers of the Antarctic embody, the narrator says, "the peculiarly human combination of curiosity and courage that has marked Antarctica's story."

The success of this project has taken the Museum in other new directions as well. Another similar enterprise is the *New Explorers* series, an alliance of public television, the Chicago public schools, several Chicago museums, and the Department of Energy. Designed to combine classroom activities, video, and museum field trips, *New Explorers* productions include half-hour segments on science and scientists, shown both on evening television broadcasts and in classrooms. The series seeks the kind of power rare for science education, stimulating curiosity with television and sustaining it with activities in school and the museums.

As the *New Explorers* series progressed, one episode with the Museum of Science and Industry as partner focused on an ambitious young scientist and the lure of space. Entitled *Endeavour 11,* after the Space Shuttle of the same name, it featured a Chicagoan, Dr. Mae Jemison, who became the first African-American woman in space. Showing intense preparations and the dramatic liftoff, the program then captured Jemison conducting biological experiments in the Shuttle laboratory. The segment effectively portrayed a working scientist under unusual circumstances. But one of the most memorable moments in *Endeavour 11* actually took place on earth after the flight. It was an assembly of several thousand high-

94

SPACE AND DEFENSE

school students from around the city, brought together to give Chicago's astronaut a rousing reception after her return from space. Addressing the students, Jemison made it plain that the road to achievement begins at an early age. "You need addition to do subtraction, you need subtraction to do multiplication," she said, and then enumerated a growing series of steps that math students must expect to master: "You need trigonometry to do calculus, you need calculus to do differential equations, you need differential equations to do partial differential equations." She paused. "And if you can't do partial differential equations, the Shuttle's not going anywhere." A cheer went up from the students in the audience, the loudest cheer anyone had heard for mathematics in a long time.

In the exhibit *Navy: Technology at Sea,* the Museum of Science and Industry tells new and complex stories about the relationship between people and machines. But in many ways, this exhibit builds upon one striking past event well known to almost anyone who has lived in Chicago for long. That is the story of the *U-505,* a captured German U-boat brought here after World War II. Displayed majestically outside the Museum since 1954, the famous submarine has become one of the institution's most familiar icons, known to generations of visitors.

Early in the war, the *U-505* was part of a highly successful German campaign to disrupt Allied shipping. By the end of 1943, however, U-boats had been thrown on the defensive, partly by the Allies' deployment of improved sonar technology in their antisubmarine campaign. This led to the capture of the *U-505* on the open seas near French West Africa.

An Allied task force pursuing the German U-boat fleet captured the *U-505* on June 4, 1944, and secretly towed it to Bermuda, where intelligence officials examined the vessel for German naval secrets.

95

The successful and fascinating effort against the U-boats was headed by U.S. Captain Daniel Gallery, whose "hunter-killer" task force made contact with the *U-505* on June 4, 1944. By doggedly trailing the sub and dropping a series of depth charges, the Americans forced it to surface and to surrender. Standing orders from the German command called for the crew to open all intake valves before abandoning ship, with the intention of sinking the vessel lest it be captured and reveal its many technological secrets. Captain Gallery, however, was determined to capture the submarine as well as its sailors. In rough waters, the Americans took the crew captive at gunpoint; then in a dramatic and dangerous move, several U.S. seamen rushed down the hatches, found the intake valves, and screwed them shut. Its seaworthiness assured, the *U-505* was hooked to a line and towed to the relatively remote port of Bermuda where it would be safe from espionage. While the German command assumed that the *U-505* was resting on the bottom, American teams inventoried the submarine stem to stern. What they found helped them, among other things, to break secret German codes, vitally important in the final Allied victory a year later.

ABOVE

Ten years after its capture, the *U-505* made a more public journey — from Portsmouth, New Hampshire, through the Great Lakes to the Museum of Science and Industry. The submarine was pulled up onto the beach as it prepared to cross 57th Street.

RIGHT

On its way from Lake Michigan to the side of the Museum, the *U-505* ran across a track of rollers.

SPACE AND DEFENSE

After the war, the *U-505* was drydocked in Portsmouth, New Hampshire, and some years later, Major Lohr of the Museum learned that the sub was about to be scrapped. Because Daniel Gallery was from Chicago, the Major reasoned that the *U-505* should by rights come to reside in the same city. An act of Congress was necessary to transfer ownership, and a local fund-raising effort was undertaken to pay for transporting the ship – by towboat up the St. Lawrence Seaway and through the Great Lakes – and refurbishing it. Between June and August 1954, the long trip was made, with the trickiest part, as everyone in Chicago became aware, being the last 800 feet on rails and rollers, up from the beach, across Lake Shore Drive, and onto the submarine's perch by the Museum's East Pavilion. This engineering feat drew a crowd of thousands; the day they closed Lake Shore Drive became one of the milestones in the Museum's history (foreshadowing the similar transit of the Museum's 727 airliner 40 years later).

97

The *U-505* stretches the entire
length of the Museum's east end.

100

OPPOSITE AND ABOVE

The exterior of the *U-505* appears
massive, yet its interior is cramped and
congested with nautical instruments.

RIGHT

At the foot of each bunk are the
U-505's torpedo chutes.

101

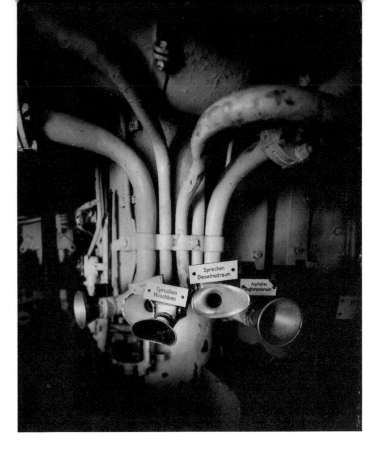

RIGHT

A collection of speaking tubes enabled the *U-505*'s crew to communicate with other sections of the ship.

BELOW

In the control room, visitors have a sense of the small spaces and the complex operations of a submarine.

The limited sleeping space on the
U-505 was accessible through this
portal.

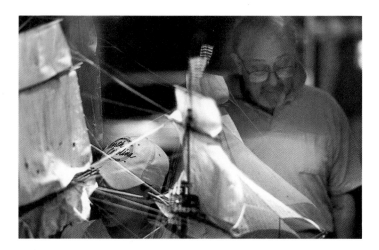

Teaching lessons about telecommunications, radar, and sonar, the exhibit *Navy: Technology at Sea* opens with a collection of ship models, followed by a walk-through replica of the U.S.S. *George Washington.*

The *U-505* has long demonstrated fundamental principles of undersea warfare. It shows the deadly torpedo tubes as well as the historical cryptographic machines that were an important part of World War II technology. As a museum exhibit, the vessel is also impressive for its paradoxical effects of scale. Seen from the outside, it looks enormous on the lawn near the Museum's old lagoon, but upon entering the ship, visitors become intensely aware of the cramped, almost claustrophobic conditions endured by submariners in the last world war. This physical sensation is an important element in an exhibit that makes many lessons of naval engineering unforgettable.

Not far from the *U-505, Navy: Technology at Sea* opened in 1994. This exhibit demonstrates the highly advanced technology developed and used by the modern Navy, while simultaneously capturing a sense of the human drama of this life at sea. Such a goal was not simple, and particularly complicated by the fact that the primary purpose of much on display in the exhibit is the application of deadly force. Dealing appropriately with the reality of warfare posed a serious challenge. If it were not faced forthrightly, the exhibit might seem shallow. If featured too prominently, it could overshadow the Museum's primary commitment to technological education.

This control room was modeled after one on the submarine U.S.S. *Chicago*.

The periscope of the model control
room based on the U.S.S. *Chicago*
looks out over the neighborhood
surrounding the Museum.

Finding such a balance had been on the minds of the Museum's exhibit staff at least since 1988, when several of them sailed on a variety of modern ships to visualize what the new exhibit might look like. These designers were impressed by an enormous technology-driven organization, with leading-edge aeronautics and telecommunications on all vessels. (They also learned of more earth-bound advances, such as Velcro, first developed for Navy flight suits.) At the same time, the designers also noted the human element. While visiting an aircraft carrier, for example, they witnessed thousands of sailors and flyers working together with remarkable efficiency, from F-15 pilots preparing for flight to machine specialists running turbine engines far below decks. "There wasn't a lot of smiling," said one member of the Museum team. "Everyone had a job to do, and they understood that the job was a matter of life and death every day." What the Museum ultimately sought to capture in its Navy exhibit was a sense of the thousands involved in complex operations, working smoothly together in sometimes-dangerous circumstances, and using some of the world's most advanced technology.

The Museum acquired many examples of this equipment to re-create that drama in the setting of a realistic exhibit. In the Museum's version of a combat control center, a web of computers and telecommunications devices shows what sailors really see as they direct carefully calibrated operations over hundreds and thousands of miles. Also remarkable are two flight simulators, using virtual reality to create lifelike scenarios for the training of fighter pilots. These simulators have quickly attained the popularity of roller coasters for many visitors, but they also convey a serious message: they show how digital technology enables the Navy to maintain a high state of readiness for the exercise of lethal power.

It was clear from the beginning that *Navy: Technology at Sea* would require updating from time to time to keep it current. As radar and stealth technologies improve, so must the exhibit. While technology always advances, however, designers are also aware that there are some things which should not change – a lesson learned from the Museum's many enduring icons.

Only time will tell which parts of the Navy hall – also the Crown Space Center and others of the Museum's most modern exhibits – will continue to speak to future visitors with the passage of time. Which objects and displays will still illuminate and inform even after they are no longer on technology's leading edge? In the Henry Crown Space Center, that unusual quality most certainly resides in the *Apollo 8* spacecraft. In the Navy exhibit, it may evolve in something as simple as the working periscope. Wherever they are to be found, however, the true icons of the future will be the objects that strike some perhaps unexpected, responsive chord in the visitor. They will come to be cherished as they reveal the very human dynamics of scientific endeavor.

107

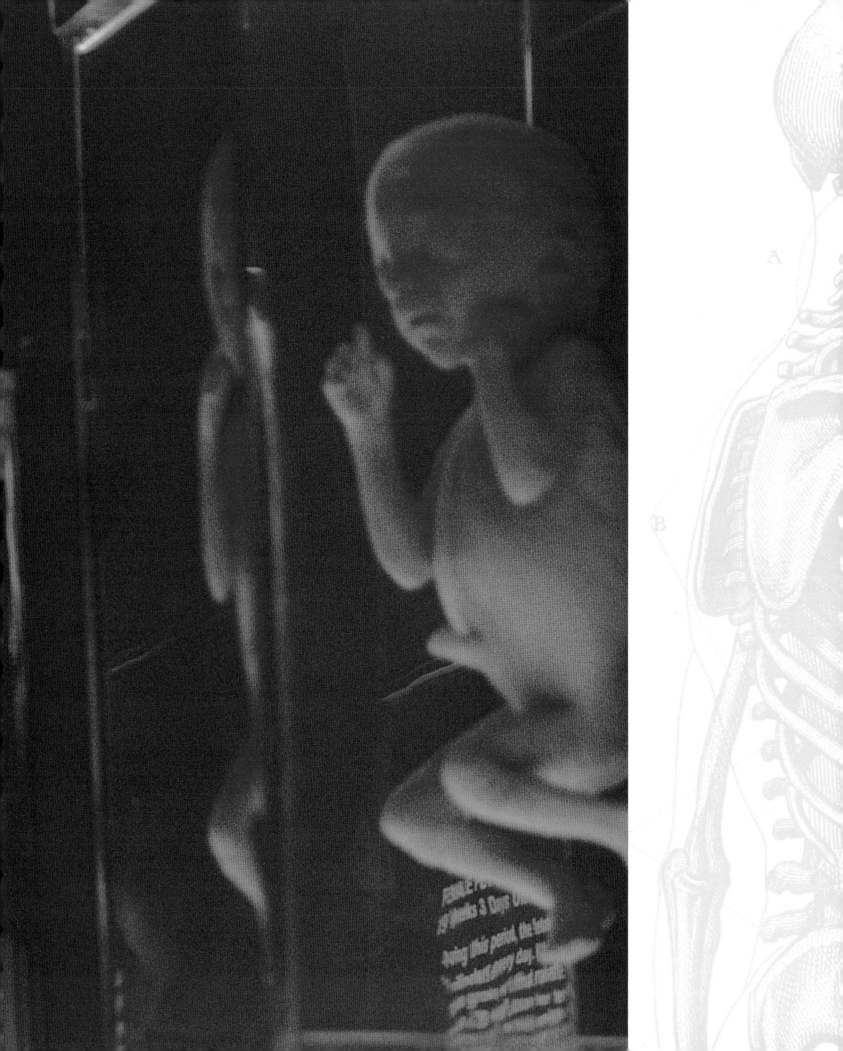

The human body, even when only represented in pictures and models, has exceptional power over our imaginations. At the Museum of Science and Industry, the body has been at the center of a number of popular exhibits; as they have focused on highly technical advances in biology and medicine, they have also revealed much about our overall understanding of ourselves and our essential humanity. These exhibits have contained some of the Museum's most powerful images, which frequently begin with the most familiar of all things – our physical selves – yet also drive the imagination toward the mysteries of what make us the way we are.

A well-known example is one of the Museum's legendary icons. Now called *Prenatal Development,* it consists of 41 actual human embryos and fetuses in successive stages of development. First installed at the Museum in 1939, this collection has never required much explanatory text to make a significant impression on visitors young or old. The exhibit illustrates with mute eloquence the way that life develops from a tiny embryo and grows, with gathering complexity, into the form of a conscious human being.

The collection prompts a rare response in the Museum – silence. In an institution known for activity and a certain amount of commotion, *Prenatal Development* draws visitors close to its row of glass cases in a kind of hush. It seems to strike deep into visitors' consciousness.

The Human Body

The *Prenatal Development* exhibit is the natural starting point of the Museum's Human Body Zone.

Prenatal Development exemplifies many characteristics that comprise an icon at the Museum of Science and Industry. It has, among other things, an evocative history. The specimens were first placed on public display at A Century of Progress in 1933 after the collection was assembled by Dr. Ruth Button, an obstetrician and one of the few female physicians in Chicago at that time.

Button served on the staff of Cook County Hospital, and her patients included many poor and indigent during the Depression. When pregnancies of women in her care ended in miscarriage, some lacked the financial means to bury their unborn children. Button asked them if the fetuses might be added to her scientific collection, and some said yes.

At the world's fair, this collection was displayed among other medical exhibits in the Hall of Science, including a wide range of medical models, illustrations of X-ray technology, and even George Washington's false teeth (in a section on dental health). The collection drew predictably large crowds, and it later came to the Museum along with many of the fair's other exhibits.

111

Prenatal Development consists of 41 human fetuses in various stages of growth, donated to the Museum by obstetrician Dr. Ruth Button in 1939. This exhibit often changes the visitor's pace to one of thoughtful observation.

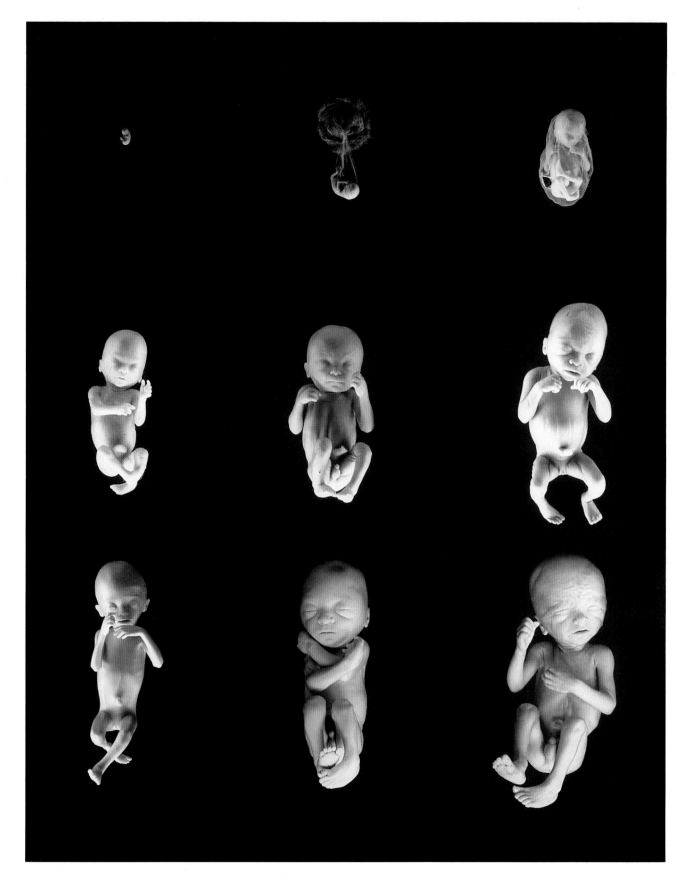

THE HUMAN BODY

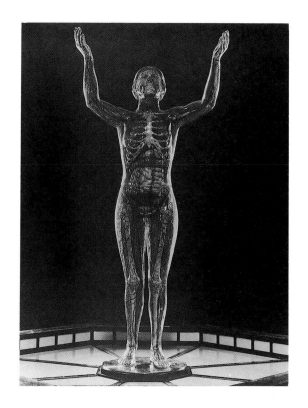

The *Transparent Woman* was a long-time exhibit at the Museum. With lights illuminating various organs as the taped script described them, it served as a centerpiece of the medical exhibits when it was completed in 1939.

OPPOSITE

The exhibit follows human development from conception to delivery. This photograph captures selected stages from 7 weeks and 6 days to 23 weeks and 1 day.

Prenatal Development has endured at the Museum as the majority of its other medical exhibits have been updated. Clearly, the exhibit captures the visitor's imagination. Parents are often seen walking their children through the exhibit, quietly explaining something of the mysteries of life. Adults, too, are often mesmerized – touched perhaps by the fragile process of the womb. Today, *Prenatal Development* remains a timeless exhibit, as powerful as ever and touching contemporary medical issues – such as abortion and sex education – in direct if delicate ways.

Like *Prenatal Development,* other notable medical displays were put on view during the early years of the Museum. By 1940, as the health and medical-science halls at the Museum were being expanded, ambitious new exhibits were devoted to medical history, X-ray technology, and a subject called "the wonders of hormone chemistry," among many others. One such exhibit was the *Transparent Woman,* which used an audio recording and changing lights to help explain the interior structures of a woman's body. As the recorded script described each organ in a sentence or two, the anatomical area in question was illuminated. The script also included snippets of medical thinking that marked the 1940s. "The amazing wonder of the human body is here revealed – more marvelous than any machine ever contrived by the ingenuity of man!"

113

Anatomical Sections, better known as "body slices," are vertical and horizontal sections of human cadavers. Strange, and to some a bit ghoulish, the exhibit serves as a vivid object lesson in human anatomy.

Besides the purely scientific, the messages contained in many medical exhibits of this period in the Museum had a social component as well. A curator at the time wrote that these efforts were designed "to demonstrate that the health of the worker and the executive is just as important as the products of industry." The same curator also noted that exhibits might "instruct the public in the intricacy of the living human machine and give warning not to meddle with it by dangerous self-medication." These goals reflected straightforward educational objectives of the Museum at the time.

Promoting personal health was the inspiration behind another Museum icon that has endured to the present day – the "walk-in" heart which was first placed among the medical exhibits in 1952. Called the "largest heart in the world," the 16-foot model was originally sponsored and created by the Chicago Heart Association at a time when many important discoveries were being made about the cardiovascular system and the causes of coronary disease. Here again, the objective of the exhibit was first to create a sense of familiarity – and curiosity – with something that most people may already know a little about, in principle at least, but almost never actually see.

Anatomically correct in form, the walk-in heart represented the commitment of the Heart Association and the Museum to scientific accuracy. Designed and constructed by the medical illustration studios at the University of Illinois in Chicago, the model enabled visitors to go inside and inspect muscle and valve structures at close range. Its builders thought that the experience might evoke a tour of Mammoth Cave. The sound effect of a beating heart added a particularly mesmerizing touch. Overall, the display demonstrated the validity of an old theorem at the Museum of Science and Industry: oversized environments fill the senses and invite visitors to investigate further. The model was accompanied by an elaborate supporting exhibit about the physiology of the cardiovascular system and the importance of informed health choices.

From the beginning, the heart exhibit used highly effective interactive techniques to engage visitors physically with the important, perhaps lifesaving, medical messages. At one of the exhibit's displays, for example, visitors were invited to squeeze a lever 70 times a minute, mimicking the heart's continuous exertion – approximately 70 contractions a minute – over the course of a lifetime. The lesson was that the heart is a powerful "engine" that does the body's hardest work; yet it is also a delicate human organ whose unremitting labor puts it under great stress. Care and attention are required to maintain its health.

115

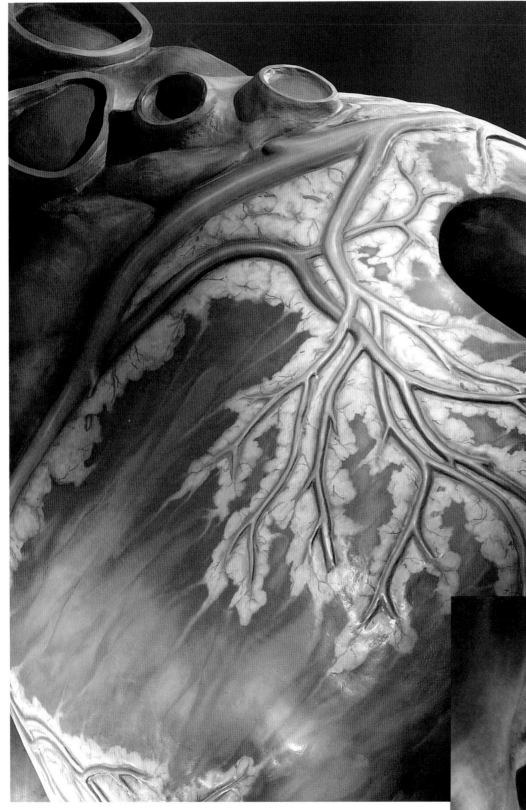

The 16-foot Giant Heart, which stands at the entrance of the Museum's exhibit on cardiovascular health, was constructed by University of Illinois medical illustrators in 1952. Likened to a trip through subterranean caves, the experience of walking among its arteries, veins, and giant muscles is unforgettable.

THE HUMAN BODY

A father and his children work with models to understand the heart's structure and function.

The early heart exhibit went on to show how certain kinds of behavior could indeed lead to a healthier heart. Toward the end of the exhibit was a push-button panel – the electrical systems here were as sophisticated as any ever before used in the Museum – with up-to-date answers to common questions about cardiovascular health.

The Heart Association continued to update the exhibit over the years and quickly included the results of additional research as it became available. By 1961, heavy users of cigarettes and people with high-fat diets (that is, over 40 percent of total calories) were placed in high-risk groups. Later, as time passed and science increased public understanding of heart disease, other risk groups were added to the exhibit. These gradual changes demonstrated the commitment of the Museum to update and change its message as new information becomes available. It also reinforced the primary role of the Museum of Science and Industry to interpret scientific research for a wide public and help to make sometimes abstract medical subjects understandable and prominent in the lives of people outside the medical profession.

117

The Museum's "icons" are those exhibits that remain ageless, continuing to delight and teach visitors for generations. One such icon was instituted in 1954, when baby chicks began hatching in the *Food For Life* hall; since then they have attracted, mesmerized, and educated countless visitors.

119

New eggs are put in the Museum's incubators daily so that visitors can observe at any time the delightful progress of a chick's hatching.

Learning and Learning Disabilities:
Explorations of the Human Brain
explains the workings of the brain
from microscopic cellular activity to
human cognitive functions such as
counting, remembering, and reading.

One of the Museum's major projects of the 1980s – an exhibit on the subject of the human brain – consolidated much of what the Museum had learned in the preceding decades about presenting difficult material to the public in a clear and compelling way. When it was completed, the exhibit represented one of the best solutions to date to the problem of devising a complex message and presenting it in clear and relatively simple terms. *Learning and Learning Disabilities: Explorations of the Human Brain,* as the exhibit is called, makes extensive use of video and interactive displays to examine the workings of the human mind. Most significantly, the exhibit penetrates the influence of neurological science on the lives of individuals and the way they function in society.

Bridging the gulf that often exists between basic science and the everyday experience of nonscientists was no simple undertaking. That of course has always been one of the overarching goals of the institution. This particular exhibit, however, tried also to demonstrate how a better understanding of science can not only bridge the gap, but actually alter people's lives and influence the way society behaves.

Opening in 1989, *Learning and Learning Disabilities* had gone through 15 years of proposals, plans, and provisional designs since its original conception. It began when a prominent Chicago neurologist, Dr. Louis Boshes, suggested to Victor Danilov, then president of the Museum, that the institution explore recent discoveries in brain research. Biologists had made significant progress in recent years, going beyond earlier concerns such as hemispheric studies. They were now exploring the intricacies of cellular activity and its enormous implications in understanding specific brain functions in detail.

121

Since the science of the brain is sometimes abstract, the exhibit emphasizes real-life situations, using videos and interactives to command the attention of visitors, who often start with little knowledge of this fascinating system.

One initial idea for the exhibit was to build a walk-through brain, something like the giant heart. Dr. Boshes, along with colleagues who supported his idea, believed that in this way, brain function could be shown in all its physical reality, as a seemingly infinite network of neurons and electrical charges responsible for everything from involuntary reflexes to the deepest emotions. Such a rendering of the brain's "circuitry" could significantly advance visitors' grasp of neurological science, Boshes believed. Unfortunately, funding for the project was not forthcoming.

The idea did not die, however. Then by the late 1970s, the Museum enjoyed some encouraging success with smaller exhibits devoted to basic scientific research, in fields such as physics, chemistry, and other subjects. Once again staff members of the Museum were intrigued by the possibility of exploring the abstract science of the brain.

Simultaneously, important friends of the Museum came forward who were also interested in the general topic of neurology, though less from a research perspective than from a clinical one. These two wealthy donors had family members with learning disabilities, and they understood in a personal way that the general public knew too little about the difficulties facing people who suffered from dyslexia, attention disorders, and other conditions.

In 1985, members of the exhibit staff began meeting with groups of people with disabilities and their parents to discuss the project and search for clues about what an effective exhibit might look like. The people in these groups were diverse in terms of age, gender, and life experience, but one of the exhibit developers began to notice something they all shared. It was the power of the emotions that they felt concerning their disabilities. Many were proud of their hard-won successes in overcoming them. Also impressive were the bonds that link people who have faced the same difficulties.

The staff came to believe that these individuals were the connecting thread of the story. Nobody understood the nature of disability better than they did. While neurological science could show how disabilities arose out of the unimaginable complexity of the brain, real people could explain something that was just as important for the public to understand – the experience of dealing with disability on a daily basis.

From this central insight, an array of videos was conceived that became the anchor for the exhibit as a whole. Some of these videos describe normal brain functions in short scenarios about counting, reading, remembering, and others. The donors in particular insisted that the exhibit should help parents recognize the difference between normal learning and learning deficits in their own children. The many aspects of disabilities, from specific symptoms to their social and psychological ramifications, were compressed into the intensely personal stories of children and adults shown on-camera. While detailed physiological information and neurological diagrams were also prepared to increase the visitor's scientific understanding, the element that made the exhibit come alive and truly open eyes was the personal, even emotional, touch of the exhibit. Ultimately, *Learning and Learning Disabilities* was less a map of the brain than a picture book of human experiences.

During the tenure of Dr. James S. Kahn as president of the Museum of Science and Industry, beginning in 1987, the Museum has expanded its commitment to difficult medical and social topics. Its most notable endeavor in this regard has been the effort to mount a major exhibit on the enormously complex subject of HIV and AIDS. AIDS is an issue of obvious importance to the population at large, yet it is fraught with daunting questions, both scientific and emotional.

Addressing medical topics in a direct way is a longtime goal of the institution. Still, as the Museum embarked on its AIDS exhibit, it was faced with a most difficult tangle of highly charged social issues, from sexual orientation to substance use. These promised a challenge, perhaps even opposition, to even the most resourceful exhibit developers. Yet the Museum regarded the project as indispensable, for Kahn and many staff members were convinced that public education could affect the course of the epidemic as powerfully as the research of scientists in the laboratory.

AIDS: The War Within, as the exhibit was called when it opened in 1995, drew heavily on the Museum's long experience with medical subjects, especially in its project on the human brain. At the same time, the AIDS exhibit demonstrates how every major undertaking encounters novel problems of its own and calls for entirely new solutions. In this instance, perhaps the most difficult issue concerned the powerful emotions associated with the disease.

AIDS: The War Within is one of the most ambitious and complete examinations of the AIDS epidemic in any museum. The project involved elaborate planning – from meeting with members of the community to designing galleries for maximum impact. Because AIDS is microscopic in nature, the virus was represented in an exaggerated form to have the requisite physical and emotional impact.

Learning in the AIDS exhibit takes place in many ways. An exhibit unit, called "Toss-a-Virus" launches soft-ball-sized viruses toward a target cell to demonstrate that HIV attaches itself to some blood cells and falls away from others.

Dr. Barry Aprison, the head of the AIDS exhibit development team, examines a model not long before exhibit construction began.

126

To understand these emotions and many other social aspects of the AIDS epidemic, the Museum staff took a page from the brain exhibit. They conducted extended discussions with groups of people involved in the fight against the disease. By communicating with a variety of organizations, and with groups of schoolchildren as well, the Museum hoped to shape an exhibit that would examine the most important scientific and social issues for the greatest number of people.

One of the most poignant moments of this planning process occurred when members of the Museum staff met with students in the seventh and eighth grades in nearby neighborhoods. They discovered, among other things, that youngsters' ideas about AIDS were an alarming mixture of fact and fiction. These students knew much terminology about the disease, including acronyms like HIV and NIH, but they also had many bizarre misconceptions. Some said they believed AIDS was the result of a medical conspiracy. Many could recite "safe sex" like a mantra but had little practical idea what it meant.

Also taking part in the AIDS exhibit planning were groups actively engaged in fighting the AIDS epidemic. Some were charitable organizations, others were militantly activist. Each articulated a particular point of view and helped sensitize the exhibit team to so-called "hot-button" issues connected with AIDS – issues as difficult as homophobia, intravenous drug use, and negative racial stereotypes. Such understanding was necessary to control the emotions that an exhibit of this kind can trigger and maintain its critical focus: medical education and containment of the epidemic.

127

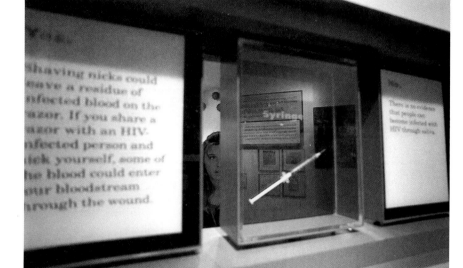

ABOVE

Interactive computer programs in the AIDS exhibit teach lessons concerning epidemiology and the other branches of medical and social science that are crucial weapons in the fight against the disease.

UPPER RIGHT

The AIDS exhibit employs various techniques to examine the truths and myths of disease transmission. These rotating panels question the visitor on which objects – including a syringe, a spoon, and a razor – could pass on the disease.

LOWER RIGHT

As with all the Museum's exhibits, members of the staff are integral components in educating the visitor.

Beyond the lessons of community involvement, exhibit developers also generated their own sparks of creativity to bring the exhibit to life. An early design decision of the team was to create the image of an invasion in the exhibit hall itself. Thus, three-dimensional HIV cells magnified to the size of softballs were attached in large random clusters to walls and columns. Large panels of super-heroes were produced to suggest that the threat of AIDS required the most formidable counteroffensive.

There were many other interesting design approaches intended to draw youngsters and adults into a subject that was as serious as death, but also offered the possibility that the disease can be defeated. In this exhibit, the dire consequences of AIDS are never far from the surface, but the primary message targets the fact that an individual can assert active control over his or her own fate.

This basic lesson is hardly simple, but it is similar to others that the Museum of Science and Industry has undertaken faithfully over the decades. Medical knowledge grows more complex, and the social implications of science and disease grow more difficult. Yet, the Museum's fundamental objective remains constant. That is to provide hard information – much of it new and sometimes controversial – for insight into ourselves and the way we live our lives.

Just as the nineteenth century ushered in the Industrial Revolution, so the twentieth century may well be remembered as the dawn of the Information Age. The machines of the digital revolution are everywhere; the constantly emerging technologies that collect, sort, transmit, and sometimes manipulate the oceans of information now at our disposal are as essential to modern life as they are, to many people, mysterious.

Since its inception, the Museum of Science and Industry has explored this world of communications and information technology. Guglielmo Marconi, inventor of the radio, was feted by the Museum's founders in 1933, and over the ensuing decades the Museum has witnessed the evolving Information Age at close range. From the telephones shown in its earliest exhibits to more recent wonders of virtual reality, the Museum has sought to explore both the changing technologies themselves and the drastic cultural changes brought on by the constant flow of new machines.

Comprehending and explaining the information revolution represents an unending challenge at the Museum. The Internet may someday seem as crude as the Model-T. Even harder to grasp are changes in the way new technologies are developed and delivered. Tomorrow's hypermedia, in whatever form they take, may come not from computer companies at all, but from your telephone-service provider, perhaps, or even an entertainment cartel. Understanding the machines that define our age proves to be an elusive goal.

Communications

A young boy experiments with the
Thermal Imaging Portal.

Nonetheless, there are strands of continuity in the development of communications technology. While technical details evolve with unimaginable complexity, certain underlying, fundamental principles can be understood through lessons close to everyday experience. An example is one of the oldest "icons" of the Museum, the *Whispering Gallery*. The exhibit dates back to 1938, the year the West Pavilion was opened and the Museum's new interior was widely praised as an Art Deco masterpiece. What was created in the *Whispering Gallery* – inspired by architecture as much as by science – was a demonstration of form serving function. Early designs for the West Pavilion defined this space as little more than a corridor connecting the Museum's Central Pavilion with its West Pavilion. Sometime during the design process, however, it was suggested that the streamlined curves of this long, narrow hallway could be used to demonstrate a basic principle of physics – the behavior of sound waves.

The *Whispering Gallery,* today as in 1938, enables a visitor at one end of the hall to hear clearly the faintest words spoken by someone at the opposite end. While the demonstration is simple, it teaches a basic lesson about communications: sound waves, which quickly fade as they spread out in space, can be reflected, concentrated, and magnified through human device. The initial "signal" is a malleable thing. It can be manipulated by many means – electrical, digital, or in this case, acoustical. The *Whispering Gallery* opens the visitor's mind to all such possibilities.

133

The *Whispering Gallery* was constructed in 1938 to demonstrate the surprising behavior of sound waves.

From the time it opened, the Museum of Science and Industry was known as an interactive museum, using current, real-life technology.

The Museum has not been alone in its desire to promote better understanding of information technology. The subject has brought many partners to the Museum – mostly private corporations seeking an audience with curiosity about the way their machines work. Among long-time sponsors in the Museum's exhibit halls, Bell Telephone came with its earliest exhibit in 1939: the memorable *Oscar the Dummy,* which the company had introduced at the Century of Progress world's fair in 1933.

"Oscar" – a mannequin dressed in an executive's clothing – inhabited a glassed-in office with an audience seated just outside. Oscar was equipped with high-sensitivity microphones in each ear. Live actors, positioned at various points inside the office, spoke and made other sounds in Oscar's presence, and as Oscar "heard," so did visitors wearing stereophonic earphones. Whispers, shouts, and even the sound of a dropped pencil were picked up so precisely and reproduced with such fidelity that people listening in felt as if they were inside Oscar's office.

Oscar the Dummy proved very popular and was considered a ground-breaking exhibit at the time. For visitors, it transmitted the message that the sense of hearing not only enables us to understand words or enjoy pleasing sounds – it also provides an intuitive awareness of ourselves in our environment. Among the Museum staff, it demonstrated that sound represents a powerful element in effective exhibits, and technology could be used as the medium as well as the message.

134

Over the years, Bell Telephone exhibits kept pace with burgeoning changes in communications. In the 1950s, a diorama in the company's elaborate new exhibit, called the *Hall of Communications,* depicted a miniature city, complete with buildings, streets, vehicles, and an extensive telephone network. To dramatize the role played by the telephone in everyday life, the diorama used phone receivers playing a tape-recorded story of an injured boy and the series of emergency calls that saved his life. While the tape told the story, visitors could also watch the story unfold as lights blinked across phone lines, vehicles moved over streets, and events reached their happy climax.

Many visitors were satisfied by this scenario and moved on. Exhibit designers believed that others would remain curious as to how the diorama worked. Thus, staff members in the exhibit were trained to explain that the moving parts of the model city were activated by a specialized communications system. The recorded narrative of the rescue story was punctuated by tones pitched higher than humans can hear. An "electric brain" sensed these tones and responded by issuing commands for each task – turning on a light or dispatching an ambulance – to be performed on cue.

Subsequent Bell exhibits often represented a substantial investment. *Picturephone* was a blockbuster when it was added to the galleries in 1964. Hooked up to other *Picturephone* devices at Disneyland in California and the Franklin Institute in Philadelphia, it allowed callers to see whom they were speaking with. The exhibit may now be remembered as a promotion for a once-promising technology that never panned out, but at the time, it helped make visitors conscious of how the field now known as "consumer electronics" would one day grow to then-unimagined dimensions. The transistors that created the miniaturized television tubes of *Picturephone* were already ushering in a vast new industry and promised a revolution in daily life.

BELOW LEFT

Picturephone was introduced in Bell Telephone's *Hall of Communications* in the mid-1960s; it enabled visitors to see Pluto in Disneyland while they were speaking with him.

BELOW RIGHT

Queen Elizabeth II visited the Museum in 1958, and with President Lenox R. Lohr as her guide, she listened to an explanation of the telephone system in the Bell Telephone exhibit.

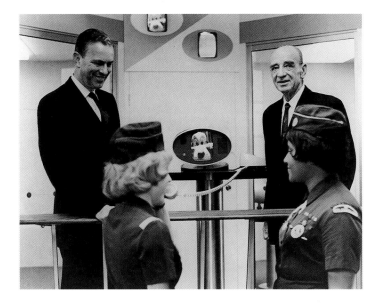

COMMUNICATIONS

The *Communications* exhibit opens
with a presentation of familiar sounds
and images commonly transmitted
via radio and television as well as a
spectrum of the more advanced
tools that connect each of us with
the rest of the world.

BELOW

Methods of voice transfer range from
these simple speaking tubes to more
complex devices.

137

Transistors were just the beginning. Their workings were relatively easy to explain, in large diagrams at the Museum which showed why and how current was amplified in telecommunications. But as the technologies of information grew increasingly powerful, and as data-handling grew more complex, machines became microscopic in scale, and their processes increasingly abstract. Quite naturally, visual presentation in the Museum became a daunting prospect.

In fact, the International Business Machines Corporation had been working on just this problem for some years. IBM president Thomas Watson, Jr., understood with rare vision that society was about to enter a vast new realm of advanced machines. He believed that employing the principles of modern design – in everything from stylish products to lucid educational exhibits – would help convey the idea of this new world. Toward that end, Watson hired some of America's most eminent designers. They not only gave visual shape to IBM's products but came up with ideas for new machines themselves: the Selectric typewriter, for instance, was first imagined not by an engineer but by a designer.

Exhibits put on view at IBM's premises were designed initially for potential customers. The audience was made up of executives in other industries who were considering the purchase of computers. When exhibits of that kind proved successful, Watson and his designers sought ways of introducing the idea of computers to the wider public. One result of this effort was *Mathematica: The World of Numbers . . . and Beyond,* which came to the Museum of Science and Industry in 1961.

Mathematica was the work of Charles Eames, now regarded as one of the foremost designers of the twentieth century. In areas ranging from furniture to films as well as exhibits, Eames's design philosophy was that useful and functional things could also be beautiful. He was famous for a plywood-molding technique, which he initially developed for making medical splints during World War II and later used to create a series of elegant chairs. Eames had a special genius for combining the useful with the visually appealing, and he applied that genius to *Mathematica.*

His objective was to penetrate the most basic level of computer technology, which he rightly judged was mathematics. Computers – which he thought of as "logic machines" – reduced the world to numerical patterns, and Eames believed that these could be captured in an array of rules and laws that were not only immutable but sometimes vastly entertaining. "One of the best-kept secrets is how unpompous scientists are at their science, and the amount of honest fun that for them is a part of it," Eames wrote. He wanted his exhibit to get that sense of fun across to the public at large.

High-tech interactives help facilitate communication among parents, children, and the exhibit.

Two boys figure out a solution to a challenge proposed by a computer program.

139

To attract and educate that public, Eames created an oversized environment to illustrate the most abstract principles. Some of the displays were quite simple, like the "Probability Machine" in which thousands of plastic balls dropped through a maze of steel pegs and settled at the bottom in what was indisputably a "bell curve." On a more cosmic scale, the physical laws to which orbiting planets are subject, called "celestial mechanics," were illustrated with steel balls rolling around and around a shallow, funnel-shaped surface. In another part of *Mathematica,* Eames used soap bubbles to illustrate how the shapes of objects are not random but formed according to calculus and the laws of "minimal surfaces."

As *Mathematica* was being installed, some staff members of the Museum were concerned. The ideas were too complicated, some said, and it seemed to have no beginning or end. Eames responded that complexity could indeed be penetrated in a skillfully wrought exhibit. He also emphasized that *Mathematica* was designed to encourage visitors to wander through it. The world, after all, is no straight-line sequence but rather a vast field of possibilities; information comes our way in random order. In *Mathematica,* Eames put his confidence in the childlike instinct for discovery.

Mathematica effectively suggested the link between fundamental science and computers, but it went beyond that. It also pointed in subtle ways to the future of microprocessors. In another section of the exhibit, Eames explained that the shapes of all natural objects – from leaves and eggs to the most extraordinary seashells – are subject to orderly, if immensely complicated, mathematical patterns. This principle underlay a development, still a decade away, wherein computers played a powerful role in the design of buildings, automobiles, and even city plans, using complex arrangements of mathematical patterns.

Mathematica broke important ground as an introduction to the ideas on which the Information Age was built. Still, as printed circuits and microchips became inconceivably small and enormously complicated, they clearly required increased attention from a museum focused on change. Even as computers were influencing our lives in the most tangible and obvious ways, their true nature and potential remained mysterious. By 1980, *Mathematica* was replaced by a more computer-intensive exhibit. Still, a penetrating exhibit about leading-edge computers remained elusive. It would be several years before the Museum harnessed resources to capture the soul of the machine.

When the Museum opened *IMAGING: The Tools of Science* in 1994, it was viewed as a landmark, not just in Chicago but in museums across the country. In a futuristic space, this exhibit demonstrates how computers can provide views of otherwise unfathomable worlds. Imaging technologies – which display normally invisible, or abstract, data – are now commonly used in fields as diverse as medicine, engineering, meteorology, and even crime detection. In some ways, computer imaging had been used in the Museum before, in touch screens and other interactive displays. But the concept of a full exhibit on the technology promised not just an array of user-friendly computers, but real insight into the relationship between advanced scientific concepts and the Information Age.

Computer imaging was introduced to the Museum in the late 1980s through a proposal from Robert N. Beck, director of the University of Chicago's Center for Imaging Science. For decades, Beck had been developing imaging technologies for a range of disciplines, primarily medicine but also other areas such as archaeology, astronomy, and even music. It was the interdisciplinary nature of Beck's proposal that immediately appealed to the Museum's president, James S. Kahn, and to his vision of the Museum as a place where the different branches of knowledge converge.

Yet the exhibit proved difficult to realize. Outside designers began working on it, and early schemes focused on commonplace objects, like trees or houses, which computers could "dissect" to illustrate inner processes (such as photosynthesis in one case and air-conditioning in the other). Ultimately, however, this plan was rejected. It showed what these remarkable tools did, but not how they did it. Moreover, the initial design missed something that was important to both the Museum and the computer: interaction with human beings.

In its final form, the *IMAGING* exhibit features a gallery filled with work stations. In one called "Seeing Sound," visitors can play music or speak near a microphone, and simultaneously view the volume, tone, or timbre of the sound transcribed in pulsating designs on a screen. In the "Morphing" station, they have computer snapshots made of their own faces, then manipulate the images in humorous or bizarre ways. In "Virtual Reality," visitors wear electronic goggles, and by turning their heads left or right, they careen through the city, head off into the countryside, and enter the "virtual" forests and mountains beyond. In each case, the exhibit provides a visible, even visceral, experience from something imaginary or abstract.

141

OPPOSITE
Starting with telephones and radios, *Communications* guides visitors all the way up to the latest and most advanced digital technologies. Here a visitor finds himself among an array of drums and other musical instruments in virtual reality.

RIGHT
Another simulation involves spreading virtual-reality paint across a screen.

143

COMMUNICATIONS

In this regard, the director of the *IMAGING* project notes that "the Museum has always been about mental *and physical* engagement." The exhibit has become a model of how this kind of engagement can be achieved. Within months of its opening, it was honored with national awards and widely praised, especially within the museum community.

To support *IMAGING: The Tools of Science* and broaden its educational reach, the Museum has added a "Mystery Lab," where the lessons of imaging technology can be explored further. New teaching methods were devised for the "Lab," where school groups use high-tech devices to solve problems as a group. Many educators believe that in such a setting outside the conventional classroom, youngsters often grasp new concepts more quickly and are eager to make discoveries on their own.

The experience of "Mystery Lab" unfolds as a scenario that begins with a video of a realistic news report. The fictional problem, described by a well-known local news anchorman, concerns a young woman who has lost consciousness at the Museum of Science and Industry. Police can find no identification on her, only a lottery ticket that turns out to have the winning numbers for a $47-million jackpot. Because the ticket is about to expire, it is urgent to discover the woman's identity, says the reporter, and a group at the Museum has been enlisted to use imaging technologies to help find out. That group, of course, is the class itself.

When the "Mystery Lab" scenario was devised by educators and designers on the Museum staff, the objective was realism. "That seems to be what is lacking in school," said one of them. "It's why so many students respond so quickly to this." As the class breaks up into groups to examine different clues, some use the computer to analyze stray animal hairs found on the mystery woman's clothing; others use baby pictures of missing persons and a computer-aging technique to project what they would look like now. In the end, the class as a whole comes back together, using technological resources, along with basic deductive reasoning, to solve the mystery.

PRECEDING PAGES

Visitors stand in the Thermal Imaging Portal, which projects the body's areas of heat concentration upon a 20-foot screen.

PRECEDING PAGES AND ABOVE
IMAGING: The Tools of Science, a ground-
breaking exhibit of the 1990s, enables
visitors to use cutting-edge imaging
technology as it is applied to a variety
of fields. Medical diagnostics, weather
forecasting, crime detection, and
special effects for the entertainment
industry are among the many applications examined in this award-winning
exhibit.

150

Teaching in new and vivid ways has always been central to the mission of the Museum of Science and Industry. The institution has pursued its educational role in many forms, including science clubs, teaching laboratories, and an ongoing dialogue with public schools. Educators at the Museum and teachers in the schools have endeavored to work closely together, especially in recent years, to make science a more vital and effective element of public education. At a time when our country has come to regard "science literacy" as a major challenge, programs such as the *New Explorers* and "Mystery Lab" have proved that the Museum of Science and Industry and places like it can go far toward overcoming educational deficits in society.

Some avenues to success in this endeavor are already well known. They were described a century ago when John Dewey of the University of Chicago transformed educational theory with his ardent belief that effective teaching must involve students' touch, sight, and muscular sense, as well as their intelligence. Dewey understood that museums are often better equipped to offer a hands-on experience than are classrooms. Even the wealthiest schools can rarely purchase the kind of equipment that is accessible to all in the exhibit halls of large institutions like this one.

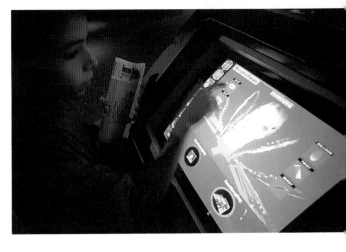

LEFT

In a hall filled with sophisticated computer-imaging systems, children can also visualize the underlying scientific principles through this low-tech liquid-crystal wall that responds to their touch.

ABOVE

In the "Face Morphing" program, visitors manipulate images of themselves captured on the computer.

151

Other avenues at the Museum are entirely new, and their future little known. Computers like those in the *IMAGING* exhibit, for example, may someday serve as teachers themselves, one-to-one tutors that will develop and adjust lessons instantly based on the response of the student. Such an approach to education corresponds closely to what educational theorist Howard Gardner calls "multiple intelligences." Many schools, Gardner states in his visionary writings, can be faulted for putting too much faith in the value of memorized facts and standardized answers. What they often miss, and the Museum clearly targets, is the many-faceted nature of problem-solving. Human intelligence has many aspects – musical, spatial, and interpersonal among many others. It implies that each individual can and should be taught in his or her own way.

The educational challenge of our society, Gardner insists, is to help students explore the kinds of problems that they can enjoy and most successfully solve. To this end, he is a great believer in museums. "Children have a chance to explore engaging materials at their own pace in their own hands-on, minds-on way," Gardner writes. "The challenge is to wed the regularity of school with the engagement genius of the youth museum."

The Museum of Science and Industry demonstrates that Gardner's view is an attainable goal. Over the years, many scientists have committed time and resources to this institution, citing childhood visits to museums of this kind as turning points in their lives. The mysteries found in great exhibit halls propelled them into careers dedicated to finding answers. To cultivate such outcomes, the Museum must continue to instill a sense of wonder, whether through the dark passages of the *Coal Mine,* the gleaming fuselage of the United 727, or still-unimagined exhibits of the future. Now and always, the best exhibits will inspire a kind of awe, create indelible memories, and lead to enduring interest.

A museum need not unravel every mystery, answer every question. It must instead encourage visitors to keep asking them. And if the answers aren't easy, so much the better. As generations of scientists can attest, the struggle simply to understand the important questions often leads to the only answers that are truly worth searching for.

153

In the *IMAGING* exhibit, large photographs are cast behind visitors to create a powerful visual environment.

ENERGY

Ehrlich, Paul R. *The Science of Ecology.* New York: Macmillan, 1987.

————. *Healing the Planet: Strategies for Resolving the Environmental Crisis.* Reading, Mass.: Addison-Wesley, 1991.

Encyclopedia of Earth System Science. Edited by William A. Nierenberg. 4 vols. San Diego: Academic Press, 1991.

Odum, Eugene P. *Ecology and Our Endangered Life-Support Systems.* Sunderland, Mass.: Sinauer Associates, 1993.

Parker, Steve. *Eyewitness Science: Electricity.* New York: Dorling Kindersley, 1992.

Stevenson, L. Harold. *The Facts on File Dictionary of Environmental Science.* New York: Facts on File, 1991.

Wood, Robert. *Physics for Kids: Forty-nine Easy Experiments with Optics.* Blue Ridge Summit, Pa.: TAB Books, 1990.

TRANSPORTATION

From Airships to Airbus: The History of Civil and Commercial Aviation. Vol. 1, *Infrastructure and Environment,* edited by William M. Leary. Vol. 2, *Pioneers and Operations,* edited by William F. Trimble. Washington, D.C.: Smithsonian Institution Press, 1995.

Johnstone, Michael. *Look Inside: Cross Sections – Planes.* New York: Dorling Kindersley, 1994.

Kisor, Henry. *Zephyr: Tracking a Dream across America.* New York: Random House, 1994.

Lopez, Donald S. *Aviation: A Smithsonian Guide.* New York: Prentice-Hall, 1995.

Moffat, Bruce. *Forty Feet Below: The Story of Chicago's Freight Tunnels.* Glendale, Calif.: Interurban Press, 1982.

————. *The "L": The Development of Chicago's Rapid Transit System, 1888–1932.* Chicago: Central Electric Railfans' Association, 1995.

Morris, Juddi. *The Harvey Girls: The Women Who Civilized the West.* New York: Walker, 1994.

Scarry, Huck. *Aboard a Steam Locomotive: A Sketchbook.* New York: Prentice-Hall, 1987.

Scharchburg, Richard P. *Carriages without Horses: J. Frank Duryea and the Birth of the American Automobile Industry.* Warrendale, Pa.: Society of Automotive Engineers, 1993.

Throckmorton, Peter, ed. *The Sea Remembers: Shipwrecks and Archeology.* New York: Weidenfeld & Nicolson, 1987.

Yepsen, Roger. *City Trains: Moving through America's Cities by Rail.* New York: Macmillan, 1993.

SPACE AND DEFENSE

Clancy, Tom. *Submarine.* New York: Berkley Publishing Group, 1993.

Damon, Thomas D. *Introduction to Space: The Science of Spaceflight.* Melbourne, Fla.: Krieger, 1995.

Gannon, Michael. *Operation Drumbeat.* New York: Harper & Row, 1990.

Launius, Robert D. *NASA: A History of the U.S. Civil Space Program.* Melbourne, Fla.: Krieger, 1994.

Miller, Ron. *The Dream Machines: An Illustrated History of the Spaceship in Art, Science, and Literature.* Melbourne, Fla.: Krieger, 1993.

Polmar, Norman. *The Naval Institute Guide to Ships and Aircraft of the U.S. Fleet.* 15th ed. Annapolis: Naval Institute Press, 1993.

The Story of the U-505. Chicago: Museum of Science and Industry, 1955.

Wilhelms, Don E. *To a Rocky Moon.* Tucson: University of Arizona Press, 1993.

THE HUMAN BODY

Fan, Hung, Ross F. Conner, and Luis P. Villarreal. *The Biology of AIDS.* 3rd ed. Boston: Jones & Bartlett, 1994.

Henig, Robin Marantz. *A Dancing Matrix: Voyages along the Viral Frontier.* New York: Knopf, 1993.

The Incredible Machine. Washington, D.C.: National Geographic Society, 1986.

Levine, Arnold J. *Viruses.* New York: Scientific American Library, 1992.

COMMUNICATIONS

Friedhoff, Richard, and William Benzon. *The Second Computer Revolution: Visualization.* New York: W. H. Freeman & Co., 1989.

Hall, Stephen S. *Mapping the Next Millennium.* New York: Random House, 1992.

Kurzweil, Raymond. *The Age of Intelligent Machines.* Cambridge, Mass.: MIT Press, 1990.

Levine, Joseph, and David Suzuki. *The Secret of Life: Redesigning the Living World.* Boston: WGBH, 1993.

Negroponte, Nicholas. *Being Digital.* New York: Knopf, 1995.

157

159

PHOTOGRAPH CREDITS

All images reproduced in this book were provided from the archives of the Museum of Science and Industry, except for line art credited herein and special photography commissioned from the following photographers:

Anthony Arciero: pp. 2–3, 4–5, 6–7, 10, 11 (center and right), 26, 27, 28–29, 30, 32, 33, 34 (below), 38–39, 46–47, 49, 53, 56–57, 72 (left), 80, 92, 100, 106, 108 (left), 110–11 (below), 116 (above), 118–19, 119 (above), 136–37, 150

Buffalo Museum of Science: p. 113

Chicago Architectural Photographing Company: pp. 22–23, 58 (left)

Christopher Barrett © Hedrich Blessing: p. 112

Dover Pictorial Archive Series, *Harter's Picture Archive for Collage and Illustration,* © 1978 Dover Publications: pp. 45, 67, 131

Dover Pictorial Archive Series, *Heck's Pictorial Archive of Nature and Science,* © 1994 Dover Publications: pp. 83, 108–9

Glen Gyssler: pp. 44, 66, 88, 89, 101, 102 (above)

© Hedrich Blessing: p. 75

Illinois Bell Telephone Company: p. 135 (right)

Jackson Souvenir Photography: p. 18

Rev. Ridell A. Kelsey: p. 96 (left)

Avis Mandel: pp. 40, 41, 42–43, 52, 58 (right), 59, 61, 62, 73, 91

(right), 102 (below), 104 (left), 110 (above), 111, 114, 116 (below), 117, 119 (below), 121, 126, 128, 130, 137 (right), 138, 139, 142, 143, 144–45, 146, 151, 152

Scott McDonald © Hedrich Blessing: pp. 1, 8, 11 (left), 14, 31, 51, 76, 77, 78, 98–99, 120, 124–25, 132, 148–49

Official United States Navy Photo: pp. 95, 103

Photo Ideas Inc.: pp. 60, 85

Bob Shimer © Hedrich Blessing: pp. 37, 38 (left), 55, 90, 91 (left), 104 (right), 105, 154–55

The artifact pictured on pages 85–86 and 88–90 is on loan from the National Air and Space Museum, Washington, D.C.